Adams
on
Adams

Adams
on
Adams

Selected and Edited by
Paul M. Zall

THE UNIVERSITY PRESS OF KENTUCKY

Publication of this volume was made possible in part by
a grant from the National Endowment for the Humanities.

Copyright © 2004 by The University Press of Kentucky
Paperback edition 2009

The University Press of Kentucky
Scholarly publisher for the Commonwealth,
serving Bellarmine University, Berea College, Centre
College of Kentucky, Eastern Kentucky University,
The Filson Historical Society, Georgetown College,
Kentucky Historical Society, Kentucky State University,
Morehead State University, Murray State University,
Northern Kentucky University, Transylvania University,
University of Kentucky, University of Louisville,
and Western Kentucky University.
All rights reserved.

Editorial and Sales Offices: The University Press of Kentucky
663 South Limestone Street, Lexington, Kentucky 40508-4008
www.kentuckypress.com

Frontispiece: From: Virginia F. Townsend, *Our Presidents* (NY: Worthington, 1889). Courtesy of Huntington Library.

Cataloging-in-Publication Data is available from
the Library of Congress.

ISBN 978-0-8131-9265-9 (pbk: acid-free paper)

This book is printed on acid-free recycled paper meeting
the requirements of the American National Standard
for Permanence in Paper for Printed Library Materials.

Manufactured in the United States of America.

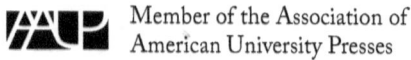

Member of the Association of
American University Presses

In memory of

William A. Moffet
Director, Huntington Library

1990–1995

Contents

Acknowledgments and Note on the Text ix
Introduction: The Last Angry Man xi
1. Becoming a Lawyer, 1735–1758 1
2. Practicing Law, 1758–1765 15
3. Becoming a Radical, 1764–1770 27
4. Reconciling Idea and Inclination, 1770–1774 41
5. Maneuvering Independence, 1774–1775 55
6. Declaring Independence, 1775–1776 67
7. Practicing Diplomacy, 1776–1780 79
8. Becoming the "Washington of Negotiation," 1781–1783 93
9. Implementing Independence, 1783–1788 107
10. Succeeding Washington, 1788–1801 121
11. Outliving Enemies, 1801–1826 137

Notes 151
Bibliography 167
Index 173

Acknowledgments

AND

Note on the Text

This selection from the writings of John Adams draws upon his letters, diaries, essays, and autobiographical sketches to tell a story of his life as he saw it. My own comments are confined to indented text. Quotations from persons other than Adams are in italics. Out of respect for The Adams Papers' copyrights, my excerpts derive from earlier texts, their various styles here made uniform.

I am truly grateful for expert advice and encouragement from George Athan Billias, William Pencak, Sally Elizabeth Glen, and John A. Schutz. Thanks also to Director David Zeidberg and to his friendly staff for care, comfort, and compassion over forty-five years in the Central Basement of the Huntington Library.

Introduction

The Last Angry Man

I first met John Adams back in the fifties when I fell in love with his wife. Along with countless casual readers, I was enthralled by their letters in the newly released Adams Papers. Next he emerged from her shadow as hero of the scholarly volumes edited by Lyman Butterfield and the very popular musical "1776." By the turn of this century, a succession of biographies culminated in David McCullough's *John Adams*, a phenomenal best-seller that made "John Adams" a household word.

Today the Web opens a ready and easy way to view a generous sampling of his writings in the Adams Papers (masshist.org/digitaladams). My selection, drawn from printed texts, lets the John Adams I know tell about his life in his own words—the best medium for discerning how he saw himself and wished us to see him.

At times Adams insisted that his was a life insignificantly lived. Other times he took great pride in having played midwife at the birth of the nation. He acted as prime mover for Independence, mobilized national resources for defense, founded the Navy, negotiated credit that financed the war and the treaties that ended it, promoted with bulldog tenacity the balance of powers and a bicameral Congress. As president he elevated the office above partisan politics, and by rejecting entangling alliances he achieved

Introduction

respect and recognition for the emerging nation. And he wrote a running record of how he did it.

From his first days in the Continental Congress, Adams wrote lively accounts of people, places, events, and feelings. Early in his career, Adams realized that "A pen is certainly an excellent instrument to fix a man's attention and to inflame his ambition."[1] He went on to write newspaper articles and pamphlets "by fits and starts for fifty or sixty years without ever correcting or revising any thing."[2] In the tranquillity of a quarter-century's retirement, he wrote reams of recollections.

As a rising young lawyer he was called upon to pen position papers for legislatures, the Continental Congress, even the Sons of Liberty. As a diplomat, he wrote such voluminous reports that Congress complained.[3] In retirement, writing became a source of therapy—"I feel at least forty years younger"[4]—and a means to salvaging a reputation from the partisan press—"I now think I was very idly employed in vindicating my conduct."[5]

When asked to write an autobiography, Adams replied that looking back would so inflame him that he would need a bucket of water by his side to put out the fires.[6] The only reason he would undertake an autobiography at all, he said, was to counter "that mass of odious abuse of my character" piled up by the press.[7] He had other excuses—carelessness and negligence in preserving papers, infirmities of old age—"sans eyes, sans hands, sans memory"[8]—and dull material—"Crimes, I thank God, I have none to record. Follies, indiscretions, and trifles enough and too many."[9]

"I am but an ordinary man," he would insist.[10] "I have one head, four limbs, and five senses, like any other man."[11] The best friend of his youth, Jonathan Sewall, remarked that Adams had none of the graces, he did not "dance, drink,

Introduction

game, flatter, promise, dress, swear with the gentlemen, or talk small talk and flirt with the ladies."[12] Adams would add that he compensated for mediocre talents with severe and incessant labor to the point of nervous breakdowns. "If I could be proud of any thing it would be industry; but even in this I am much more inclined to be ashamed that I have done no more than to be proud of what I have done."[13]

Yet Adams realized that a quick temper was a character flaw. "Some great events, some cutting expressions, some mean hypocrisies, have, at times, thrown this assemblage of sloth, sleep, and littleness into rage a little like a lion."[14] He would insist that his temper, normally "tranquil," could be triggered by "extraordinary madness, deceit, hypocrisy, ingratitude, treachery or perfidy," and even then last for only a short time.[15]

Governor Thomas Hutchinson, one of Adams's earliest public enemies, blamed that temper on jealous pride: "He could not look with complacency upon any man [with] more wealth, more honour, or more knowledge than himself." Adams, he said, would take offense at "any real or supposed personal neglect or injury."[16]

Carried to excess, Adams's candor risked ruin. French Foreign Minister Charles Gravier Vergennes could put up with Adams's "too ardent imagination and stubborness" but not with outrageous demands sent as threats.[17] No wonder Benjamin Franklin warned Congress that "the ravings of a certain mischievous madman" threatened the Franco-American alliance.[18] Thomas Jefferson echoed Franklin in saying that Adams was "always an honest man, often a great one, but sometimes absolutely mad."[19]

At one time or another, Adams's anger made enemies of both Franklin and Jefferson, along with Hutchinson, Vergennes, John Dickinson, King George III, Alexander

Introduction

Hamilton, and Mercy Warren. He wrote that Hamilton was "a bastard brat of a Scotch pedlar,"[20] Thomas Paine's *Common Sense,* "a poor ignorant, malicious, short-sighted, crapulous mass,"[21] and Paine himself, "a mongrel between pigg and puppy, begotten by a wild boar on a bitch wolf."[22] With his longevity he might have been called "the last angry man."

He created formidable enemies by wearing down opponents in debate and in writing. In anger bordering on hysteria he attacked old friend Mercy Otis Warren for her 1806 history of the Revolution. He charged her with defamation in accusing him of corrupting Revolutionary ideals for personal glory.

As if overflowing with rage pent up for years, he erupted in ten shrill letters. Three months of his "rancor, indecency, and vulgarism" wore out Warren.[23] The momentum of writing to her led to three more years of his writing weekly columns for the Boston *Patriot* (1809–1812). Reenacting a quarter-century's public service served as a kind of polemical catharsis.

Because Adams composed at white heat without revising in cold blood, his writing caused trouble. The British intercepted his private letter calling conservative leader John Dickinson, "a piddling genius" and used it for propaganda against the movement for Independence. He later blamed an inflamed temper for the "negligent, unstudied, unpolished" style of "Defence of the Constitutions of the United States," a style nevertheless important in shaping the Constitution.[24] For intemperately damning equality in "Discourses on Davila," he was branded "aristocrat" and "monarchist."

Yet, contemporaries praised Adams's public speaking. Jefferson spoke of it with reverence. Neither graceful nor fluent, Adams in 1776 was a "Colossus on the floor ... [who]

Introduction

moved us from our seats."[25] His "confident and fervid addresses... encouraged and supported us through the difficulties that surrounded us."[26]

Oddly, Adams's private conversation may have been far less confrontational than what he would sometimes have us believe. He dramatizes a bold scene in an audience with George III. The same scene described by an eyewitness says that Adams, "not a little confused," said "not a word."[27] A similar episode reveals a much lighter side of John Adams. He is awed into silence on meeting King Louis XVI, so much so that his majesty inquires whether he can speak French and then whether Monsieur Adams spoke *at all.*[28] Angry words Adams attributed to carelessness,[29] his levity to spontaneity—"It comes of itself."[30] He preferred to laugh "as the words flowed" from the heart rather than the head.[31] In a biting image, he describes posterity's view of the American revolution: "Dr. Franklin's electrical rod smote the earth and out sprung General Washington."[32]

"I cannot contemplate human affairs," he said, "without laughing or crying. I choose to laugh."[33] He thought Americans "the silliest people under Heaven" and did not exclude himself.[34] He laughed at himself recalling Europeans' certainty that he was Sam Adams, author of *Common Sense,* or puzzling over London streets named after himself, or puffing dutifully on a water pipe for diplomacy's sake. Jefferson must have had in mind the Adams who could laugh at himself when he said of Adams that to know him was to love him.[35]

Adams's casual writing style was more like conversation overheard: direct, self-dramatizing, and colloquial, even aphoristic—"A boy of fifteen who is not a democrat is good for nothing and he is no better who is a democrat at twenty."[36] He captured the sound of everyday dialogue, as

Introduction

when a dandy asks a milkmaid for a little "jigging" (in the sexual sense). The milkmaid asks, "What is that?" The dandy says, "It will make you fat!" And she replies, "Pray, jigg my mare."[37]

Adams's diaries show how he cultivated this seemingly artless art. He would practice transcribing stories he heard and add directions on how to tell them. In jest, he said this was to develop such social graces as "the nobler arts of smut, double entendre, and mimicry of Dutchmen and Negroes."[38] When teased about a rumor that C.C. Pinckney was sent to hire four girls in Europe, "two for me and two for himself," President Adams quipped, "If this be true, General Pinckney has kept them all for himself."[39]

This lively conversational style is to be expected in diaries; Adams used it in all but formal writings. The voice persuading Jonathan Sewall to write against the Writs of Assistance sounds just like the voice persuading Jefferson to write the Declaration of Independence. Or like the voice of a reluctant president-elect: "I hate speeches, messages, addresses and answers, proclamations and such affected, studied, constrained things . . . I hate to speak to a thousand people to whom I have nothing to say."[40]

We hear the same voice addressing his beloved children: "Work, you rogues, and be free. Daughter! get you an honest man for a husband and keep him honest."[41] By contrast, asked to send a toast for Boston's Fourth of July celebration in 1826, Adams gave, "Independence forever," but he added sternly, "not a syllable more."[42] All passion spent, he had already told Americans what they needed to hear.

It did not matter to him whether anyone was listening. He lived by the word and would die by the word. The writing would remain. Trying to explain what drove him so relentlessly, Adams said, "I was borne along by an irresistible

Introduction

sense of duty."[43] Duty to him was no abstraction but a willingness to set aside personal satisfaction, even family and fortune, for "a pious and a philosophical resignation to the voice of the people" who recognized his worth in calling him to serve.[44]

Nevertheless, he was reluctant to face such press abuse as had driven Washington from office. "I don't love slight, neglect, contempt, disgrace, nor insult,"[45] such as being called "Old, querulous, bald, blind, crippled, toothless Adams."[46] He served to preserve and protect the nation from Jefferson's democrats, rejecting their demands for equality. Even in the best of democracies some men were more equal than others. Based on his own experience earned in twenty-six years of national service, Adams embraced neither the perfectibility of man nor the "total and universal depravity of human nature,"[47] and he rejected democracy based on equality without regard for the basic right to rise—as he himself had risen from farmer to president.

John Adams found peace at last in the love and laughter of grandchildren and youthful neighbors, and in corresponding with old friend Jefferson on art, science, literature, history, death and dying. Both would go gently out of this world, Jefferson like a philosopher and Adams like a good soldier. "I think myself so well drilled and disciplined a soldier as to be willing to obey the word of command whenever it shall come."[48]

In the end, according to family tradition, civility prevailed. Ninety-one-year-old John Adams insisted on riding out to repay a neighbor visit. At six o'clock in the evening of the Fourth of July, 1826, the ride proved fatal. Adams did not know his old friend had died a few hours previous. As Adams died he sighed, "Thomas Jefferson" and not a syllable more.[49]

1

BECOMING A LAWYER

1735—1758

You have no idea of the prolific quality of the New England Adamses. Why, we have contributed more to the population of north America, and cut down more trees, than any other race.[1]

My father was John Adams, the son of Joseph Adams, the son of another Joseph Adams, who all lived independent New England farmers, and died and lie buried in this town of Quincy, formerly called Braintree[2].... [He] had a good education, though not at college ... was an officer of militia, afterwards a deacon of the church, and a selectman of the town; almost all the business of the town being managed by him in that department for twenty years together ... [He was] much esteemed and beloved, wherever he was known, which was not far, his sphere of life being not extensive.[3]

[He] married Susanna Boylston in October 1734, and on the [thirtieth] of October, 1735, I was born.

> At John Adams's birth, his father was forty-four, his mother twenty-six. Widowed in 1761 and dying in April 1797 at almost ninety, she lived to see the eldest of her three sons become president.

As my parents were both fond of reading and my father had destined his first born, long before his birth, to a public education I was very early taught to read at home and at a school of Mrs. Belcher, the mother of Deacon Moses Belcher, who lived in the next house on the opposite side of the road[4] ... [then] at the public Latin school.[5]

Lemuel Bryant was my parish priest, and Joseph Cleverley my Latin schoolmaster. Lemuel was a jocular and liberal scholar and divine, Joseph a scholar and a gentleman, but a bigoted Episcopalian. ... The parson and the pedagogue lived much together, but were eternally disputing about government and religion. One day when the schoolmaster had been more than commonly fanatical, and declared, "if he were a monarch, he would have but one religion in his dominions," the parson cooly replied, "Cleverley! you would be the best man in the world, if you had no religion."[6]

> Apparently the thirty-eight-year-old schoolmaster spent more class time writing sermons than teaching Latin.

Under my first Latin master, who was a churl, I spent my time in shooting, skating, swimming, flying kites, and every other boyish exercise and diversion I could invent. Never mischievous.[7]

There was a numerous family [of Indians] whose wigwam was within a mile of this house. This family were frequently at my father's house, and I, in my boyish rambles, used to call at their wigwam, where I never failed to be treated with whortleberries, blackberries, strawberries, or apples, plums, peaches, etc., for they had planted a variety of fruit trees about them.[8]

Little boats, watermills, windmills, whirligigs, birds' eggs, bows and arrows, guns, singing, pricking tunes, girls,

Becoming a Lawyer

etc.... By a constant dissipation among amusements in my childhood... my mind [lay] uncultivated.[9]

Even in old age, Adams would enjoy reminiscing about the event that changed his mind about schooling.

I had to study the Latin-grammar; but it was dull and I hated it. My father was anxious to send me to College, and therefore I studied the grammar till I could bear with it no longer; and going to my father, I told him I did not like study, and asked for some other employment. It was opposing his wishes, and he was quick in his answer.

"Well, John," said he, "if Latin-grammar does not suit you, you may try ditching, perhaps that will. My meadow yonder needs a ditch, and you may put by Latin and try that."

This seemed a delightful change, and to the meadow I went. But I soon found ditching harder than Latin, and the first forenoon was the longest I ever experienced. That day I eat the bread of labor, and glad I was when night came on.

That night I made comparison between Latin-grammar and ditching, but said not a word about it. I dug the next forenoon, and wanted to return to Latin at dinner, but it was humiliating, and I could not do it. At night toil conquered pride, and I told my father, one of the severest trials of my life, that, if he chose, I would go back to Latin-grammar.[10]

His father sent him to a conscientious private schoolmaster, Joseph Marsh. Forty-year-old Marsh, who had conducted the town school from 1731 to 1743, now lived in the old parsonage.[11]

Under my second master, who was kind, I began to love my books and neglect my sports.[12] Mr. Marsh was a son of our former minister of that name, who kept a private boarding school but two doors from my father's.... and I began to study in earnest. My father soon observed the relaxation of my zeal for fowling piece, and my daily increasing attention to my books. In a little more than a year Mr. Marsh pronounced me fitted for college.

> At age fifteen and three quarters, Adams felt frightened at the prospect of a Harvard entrance examination.

On the day appointed at Cambridge for the examination of candidates for admission I mounted my horse and called upon Mr. Marsh, who was to go with me. The weather was dull and threatened rain. Mr. Marsh said he was unwell and afraid to go out. I must therefore go alone. Thunderstruck at this unforeseen disappointment, and terrified at the thought of introducing myself to such great men as the President and Fellows of a college, I at first resolved to return home; but foreseeing the grief of my father and apprehending he would not only be offended with me but my master too whom I sincerely loved, I aroused myself, and collected resolution enough to proceed.

> The dozen miles to Cambridge on a darkening day would have been dismal. Adams's horse knew the way, but the Boston–Plymouth road of muck and mire led along the shore where menacing waves would have mimicked the turmoil of Adams's mind.

Although Mr. Marsh had assured me that he had seen one of the tutors the last week and had said to him all that was proper for him to say if he should go to Cambridge, that he was not afraid to trust me to an examination and was confident I should acquit myself well and be honourably admitted; yet I had not the same confidence in myself and suffered a melancholy journey.

Arrived at Cambridge.... Mr. [Joseph] Mayhew into

Becoming a Lawyer

whose class we were to be admitted, presented me a passage of English to translate into Latin. It was long, and casting my eye over it I found several words the Latin for which did not occur to my memory. Thinking that I must translate it without a dictionary, I was in a great fright and expected to be turned by, an event that I dreaded above all things.

Mr. Mayhew went into his study and bid me follow him. "There, child," said he, "is a dictionary, there a grammar, and there paper, pen and ink, and you may take your own time." This was joyful news to me and I then thought my admission safe. The Latin was soon made. I was declared admitted and a theme given me to write on in the vacation. I was as light when I came home as I had been heavy when I went: my master was well pleased and my parents happy.[13]

I spent the vacation not very profitably chiefly in reading magazines and a British Apollo.

> The *British Apollo* was a disreputable four-page London weekly with articles on "How many f[ar]ts to an ounce"[14] along with scandal and occasional serious pieces. His roommate in Massachusetts Hall 19, Joseph Stockbridge, could afford to dine off-campus;[15] Adams persuaded himself that dining in the Commons was more convivial.

The almost universal health among the students, was to be ascribed, next to early rising and beef and mutton pies at Commons, to the very moderate use of wine and ardent spirits. When our barrels and bottles in the Cellar were empty, we used to size [charge] it at the Buttery, and I never shall forget, how refreshing and salubrious we found it, hard as it often was.[16]

I was a mighty metaphysician, at least I thought myself such, and [classmates] thought me so too, for we were forever disputing, though in great good humor.[17] I soon became intimate with them, and began to feel a desire to equal them in science and literature. In the sciences especially mathematicks, I soon surpassed them, mainly because, intending to go into the pulpit, they thought divinity and the classics of more importance to them.[18]

Between the years 1751, when I entered, and 1754, when I left college, a controversy was carried on between [Lemuel Briant], the minister of our parish, and some of his people, partly on account of his principles, which were called Arminian, and partly on account of his conduct, which was too gay and light, if not immoral.[19]

> Reacting to the excessive zeal of the Great Awakening, Briant mocked the orthodox dogma—that our fate is predestined and salvation is through faith alone—as denying the goodness of God. When Briant's wife left him because of "several scandalous sins," rumors indicted him for "intemperance, gaming, neglect of family duties."[20]

I read all the pamphlets and many other writings on the same subjects, and found myself involved in difficulties beyond my powers of decision. At the same time, I saw such a spirit of dogmatism and bigotry in clergy and laity, that ... I perceived very clearly, as I thought, that the study of theology, and the pursuit of it as a profession, would involve me in endless altercations, and make my life miserable, without any prospect of doing any good to my fellow-men.[21]

The longer I lived, and the more experience of [clergy], and of the real design of their institution [I had], the more objections I found in my own mind to that course of life. ... I have the pain to know more than one, who has a sleepy stupid soul, who has spent more of his waking hours in darning his stockings, smoking his pipe, or playing with his fingers than in reading, conversation or reflection, cry'd

Becoming a Lawyer

up as promising young men, pious and orthodox youths and admirable preachers. As far as I can observe, people are not disposed to inquire for piety, integrity, good sense or learning in a young preacher, but for stupidity (for so I must call the pretended sanctity of some absolute dunces), irresistible grace, and original sin.[22]

I was like a boy in a carrefour [crossroads] in a wilderness in a strange country, with half a dozen roads before him groping in a dark night to find which he ought to take. ... farming, merchandize, seas, and above all war. Nothing but want of interest and patronage prevented me from inlisting in the Army. Could I have obtained a troop of horse or a company of foot I should infallibly have been a soldier. It is a problem in my mind to this day whether I should have been a coward or a hero.[23]

The last two years of my residence at college produced a club of students (I never knew the history of the first rise of it) who invited me to become one of them. Their plan was to spend their evenings together in reading any new publications, or any poetry or dramatic compositions that might fall in their way. I was as often requested to read as any other, especially tragedies, and it was whispered to me and circulated among others that I had some faculty for public speaking, and that I should make a better lawyer than divine....

My inclination was soon fixed upon the law.... It would not be difficult to remove any objections [my father] might make to my pursuit of physics or law, or any other reasonable course. My mother, although a pious woman, I knew had no partiality for the life of a clergyman. But ... a lawyer must have a fee for taking me into his office. I must be boarded and clothed for several years. I had no money; and my father, having three sons, had done as much for me, in the expenses of my education, as his estate and circumstances could justify, and as my reason or my honor would allow me to ask.[24]

Many compliments from my academical companions, who endeavored to make me believe that I had a voice and a tongue, as well as a face and front, for a public speaker [convinced me] that I was better fitted for the bar than the pulpit.[25] The noise and bustle of the courts, and the labour of inquiring into and pleading dry and difficult cases, have very few charms in my eyes. The study of law is indeed an avenue to the more important offices of the state, and the happiness of human society is an object worth the pursuit of any man. But the acquisition of these important offices depends upon many circumstances of birth and fortune, which I [had] not, that I [could] have no hopes of being usefull that way.[26]

I therefore gave out that I would take a school, and took my degree at college undetermined whether I should study divinity, law, or physic.[27] Mr. [Thaddeus] Maccarty, a clergyman of Worcester, authorized by the selectmen, at the commencement at college, in 1755, happening to be pleased with the performance of my part [as a respondent] in the public exhibition, engaged me to take the charge of the Latin school in that town. About three weeks after commencement in [August], when I was not yet twenty years of age, a horse was sent me from Worcester, and a man to attend me. We made the journey, about sixty miles, in one day, and I entered on my office.[28]

> Adams missed the joys of learning and "other pleasures" at Harvard—"singing, dancing, wooing the widow, playing cards, etc.," sometimes until two in the morning.[29] For solace he wrote to other classmates who were also teaching.

Becoming a Lawyer

[Worcester, 2 September 1755.] Sometimes paper, sometimes his penknife, now birch, now arithmetic, now a ferule, then A B C, then scolding, then flattering, then thwacking, calls for the pedagogue's attention.[30]

> One pupil said that Adams emulated Joseph Cleverley in writing rather than teaching: "He used to sit at his desk . . . nearly all his time, engaged in writing something. . . . He seemed, when not actually writing, absorbed in profound thought, and abstracted from any thing about him—and he kept the school along, by setting one schollar to teach another."[31]

[Worcester, January I know not what day 1756] I am confined myself to a like place of torment. When I compare the gay, the delightsome scenes of Harvard, with the harsh and barbarous nature of sounds that now constantly grate my ears I can hardly imagine myself the same being, that once listened to Mr. Mayhew's Instructions, and revelled in all the other pleasures of accademical life. Total and compleat misery has succeeded so suddenly to total and compleat happiness, that all the Phylosophy, I can muster can scarce support me under the amazing shock. However one source of pleasure is left me still and that is the letters of my friends.[32]

> For the next half-dozen years he would write random monologues, even dialogues, dramatizing his predicament.

1756. March 15. I sometimes in my sprightly moments consider myself, in my great chair at school, as some dictator at the head of a commonwealth. . . . I have several renowned generals but three feet high, and several deep projecting politicians in petticoats. I have others catching and dissecting flies, accumulating pebbles, cockle shells, etc. with as ardent curiosity as any virtuoso in the Royal Society. . . .

At one table sits Mr. Insipid, foppling and fluttering, spinning his whirligig, or playing with his fingers, as gaily and wittily as any frenchified coxcomb brandishes his cane or rattles his snuff-box. At another sits the polemical divine, plodding and wrangling in his mind about "Adam's fall, in which we sinned all," as his Primer has it. In short, my little school, like the great world, is made up of kings, politicians, divines, LLDs [Doctors of Laws], fops, buffoons, fiddlers, sycophants, fools, coxcombs, chimney sweepers, and every other character drawn in history, or seen in the world. . . .

Let others waste their bloom of life at the card or billiard table among rakes and fools, and when their minds are sufficiently fretted with losses, and inflamed by wine, ramble through the streets assaulting innocent people, breaking windows, or debauching young girls. I envy not their exalted happiness. I had rather sit in school and consider which of my pupils will turn out in his future life a hero, and which a rake, which a philosopher, and which a parasite, than change breasts with them, though possessed of twenty laced waistcoats and a thousand pounds a year.[33]

> Adams was still uncertain and making a choice of life seemed dependent on his immediate circumstances.

During the second quarter, the Selectmen procured lodgings for me at Dr. Nahum Willard's. This physician had a large practice, a good reputation for skill, and a pretty library . . . I read a good deal in these books and entertained many thoughts of becoming a physician or surgeon.[34] For the faculty of medicine I never had any inclination, having an aversion to sick rooms and no fondness for rising at all hours of the night to visit patients.[35]

The law attracted my attention more and more, and, attending the courts of justice . . . I felt myself irresistibly

Becoming a Lawyer

impelled to make some effort to accomplish my wishes. I made a visit to Mr. [James] Putnam,[36] a counsellor at law in very large practice and of very respectable talents and information,[37] and offered myself to him; he received me with politeness and even kindness, took a few days to consider of it, and then informed me that Mrs. Putnam had consented that I should board in the house; that I should pay no more than the sum allowed for my lodgings, and that I should pay him a hundred dollars when I should find it convenient. I agreed to his proposals, without hesitation, and immediately took possession of his office.[38]

Here, as I boarded in his family, I had the opportunities of conversing with all the judges, lawyers, and many others of the principal characters of the province, and heard their speculations upon public affairs. This was highly delightful to me, because my father, who had a public soul, had drawn my attention to public affairs. From my earliest infancy I had listened with eagerness to his conversation with his friends during the whole expedition to Cape Breton, in 1745, and I had received very grievous impressions of the injustice and ingratitude of Great Britain towards New England in that transaction, as well as many others before and after it . . . which were daily discussed in Mr. Putnam's family. [They] gave me such a disgust of the British government, that I heartily wished the two countries were separated for ever.[39]

> While persevering in the schoolroom and studying law for the next two years, Adams still could not settle on a choice between law and preaching. In the spring of 1758, Harvard awarded him an M.A., virtually a license to preach. For his health, however, he left Worcester to study for the bar at home in Braintree, and there was beset by distractions.

Braintree, 5 October 1758. Few of my contemporar beginners in the study of the law have the resolution to aim at much knowledge in the civil law; let me, therefore, distinguish myself from them by the study of the civil law in its native languages, those of Greece and Rome.... I have read about ten pages in Justinian [*Institutions*] and translated four pages into English; this is the whole of my day's work. I have smoked, chatted, trifled, loitered away this whole day almost;—by much the greatest part of this day has been spent in unloading a cart, in cutting oven wood, in making and recruiting my own fire, in eating victuals and apples, in drinking tea, cutting and smoking tobacco, and in chatting with Dr. Savil's wife at their house and at this. Chores, chat, tobacco, tea, steal away time.[40]

> Anticipating another examination, Adams was anxious, "shy, under awe and concern," and sought counsel from attorney general Jeremiah Gridley in Boston.

Boston, 25 November 1758. Went in the morning to Mr. Gridley's and asked the favor of his advice, what steps to take for an introduction to the practice of law in this county. He answered, "Get sworn."

Ego.—But in order to [do] that, sir, as I have no patron—

Gridley—I will recommend you to the court. Mark the day the court adjourns to, in order to make up judgments. Come to town that day, and, in the mean time, I will speak to the bar, for the bar must be consulted, because the court always inquires if it be the consent of the bar.

> Gridley interrogated him on what he had studied and assigned him reading on common, civil, and admiralty law. He also advised twenty-three-year-old Adams about the practice of law and professional life.

"I have a few pieces of advice to give you, Mr. Adams. One is to pursue the study of the law, rather than the gain

Becoming a Lawyer

of it; pursue the gain of it enough to keep out of the briers, but give your main attention to the study of it. The next is, not to marry early, for an early marriage will obstruct your improvement; and, in the next place, it will involve you in expense. Another thing is, not to keep much company, for the application of a man who aims to be a lawyer must be incessant; his attention to his books must be constant, which is inconsistent with keeping much company."

> Subtly seeking praise for having read legal history in original languages, Adams found he had wasted his time.

I asked his advice about studying Greek. He answered, "It is a matter of mere curiosity."

> After interviewing another member of the bar, Adams spent the weekend "in absolute idleness, or, which is worse, gallanting the girls." On Monday, 6 November, along with his friend Samuel Quincy, he was formally admitted to practice in the lower county court.

After the oath, Mr. Gridley took me by the hand, wished me much joy, and recommended me to the bar. I shook hands with the bar, and received their congratulations, and invited them over to Stone's to drink some punch, where the most of us resorted, and had a very cheerful chat.[41]

> Robert Stone's Royal Exchange Tavern would be the scene of two more events critical in Adams's career. The Boston Massacre would take place in front of the building, and the Boston Tea Party would be launched from its meeting room.[42]

2

PRACTICING LAW

1758–1765

Worcester friends urged him to stay. Adams, ill from overwork, homesick, facing an uncertain future, sought the solace of his parents' home. The family's 140 acres extended from the busy Boston–Plymouth road to the foot of granite-laced Penn's Hill. Braintree, twelve miles from Boston, no mere crossroads village, boasted about four hundred solid, two-story houses of cracker-box design—with thick walls of brick and clay sheathed in wood, roofs slanting almost to the ground, windows opening to breezes from the sea.[1]

There was one motive with me which was decisive. I was in very ill health . . . I panted for want of the breezes from the sea, and the pure zephyrs from the rocky mountains of my native town; that my father and mother invited me to live with them; and, as there never had been a lawyer in any country part of the then county of Suffolk, I was determined at least to look into it and see if there was any chance for me.[2]

In the beginning Adams found only frustration and failure. Competition came not from Boston lawyers but from pettifoggers, amateurs who clogged the country courts with frivolous litigation. Having read legal theory and history when he should have been learning how to practice law, he lost his first case because he did not even know how to draw a writ. He blamed the failure on his mentor, external pressures, and ultimately himself.

Monday, 18 December 1758. I was obliged to finish it without sufficient examination. If it should escape an abatement, it is quite undigested and unclerk-like. I am ashamed of it, and concerned for it. If my first writ should be abated, if I should throw a large bill of costs on my first client, my character and business will suffer greatly; it will be said, I do not understand my business.... I hope the dispute will be settled between them, or submitted, and so my writ never come to an examination.

Friday, 29 December 1758. Let me note the fatal consequences of precipitation. My first determination, what to do in this affair, was right; I determined not to meddle, but, by the cruel reproaches of my mother, by the importunities of [client] Field, and by the fear of having it thought I was incapable of drawing the writ, I was seduced from that determination; and what is the consequence? the writ is defective. It will be said I undertook the case, but was unable to manage it; this nonsuit will be in the mouth of everybody.... Let me never undertake to draw a writ without sufficient time to examine and digest in my mind all the doubts queries, objections, that may arise.

> When the court dismissed his second case, Adams blamed pettifoggers for initiating the action in the first place. But he was unprepared mentally or temperamentally to deal with their disorderly conduct.

Practicing Law

Wednesday, 3 January 1759. Yesterday, went down to defend an action for an old horse against Samuel Spear [for selling an old horse that died soon after]. This was undertaking the relief of distressed poverty; the defence of innocence and justice against oppression and injustice.... I did not clearly understand the case, had no time to prepare, to fix in my mind, beforehand, the steps that I should take.... It was a scene of absolute confusion ... the parties raging and scolding, I arguing; and the three [pettifoggers] proposing each one his project; and all the spectators smiling, whispering, etc. My attention was dissipated, and I committed oversights, omissions, inexpert management.... If Spear had applied to such as knew, he would not have brought the writ; but deputy sheriffs, petit justices, and pettifogging meddlers, attempt to draw writs, and draw them wrong oftener than they do right. They are meddlers, hinters, and projectors. I should have made a motion to the justice, that either the defendant, or I, might be consulted in the settlement of this affair, and that [they] who had no concern with it, might not determine it as they pleased.³

> Angered by such disorder in the courts, Adams sought help in reforming the system, especially with regulating pettifoggers. He turned to elder members of the Boston bar and, by design or not, attracted their notice as a young man anxious about respect for law and lawyers.

Looking about me in the country, I found the practice of law was grasped into the hands of deputy sheriffs, pettifoggers, and even constables, who filled all the writs upon bonds, promissory notes, and accounts, received the fees established for lawyers, and stirred up many unnecessary suits. I mentioned this to some of the gentlemen in Boston, who disapproved and even resented them very highly. I asked them whether some measures might not be agreed upon at the bar, and sanctioned by the court, which might remedy the evil. They thought it not only practicable, but highly expedient, and proposed meetings of the bar to deliberate upon it. . . . Many of these meetings were the most delightful entertainments I ever enjoyed.[4]

> His network of friends spread along with his practice. Still unsure of himself, he acquired the traditional practice of daily self-examination—"What good or ill have I done this day? Where have I failed and in what way?" To vary the routine and also improve his writing, he composed debates, as with the goddess "Virtue."

Virtue: Which, dear youth, will you prefer, a life of effeminacy, indolence and obscurity, or a life of industry, temperance and honor? Take my advice . . . return to your studies, and bend your whole soul to the institutes of the law and the reports of cases that have been adjudged by the rules in the institutes; let no trifling diversion, or amusement, or company, decoy you from your book; that is, let no girl, no gun, no cards, no flutes, no violins, no dress, no tobacco, no laziness, decoy you from your books.

[Adams:] Laziness, languor, inattention, are my bane. I am too lazy to rise early and make a fire; and when my fire is made, at ten o'clock my passion for knowledge, fame, fortune, for any good, is too languid to make me apply with spirit to my books, and by reason of my inattention my mind is liable to be called off from law by a girl, a pipe, a poem, a love-letter, a *Spectator*, a play, etc. etc.

[Virtue:] But keep your law book or some point of law in your mind, at least, six hours in a day.

[Adams:] I grow too minute and lengthy. . . . What am I doing? shall I sleep away my whole 70 years? no, by every thing I swear I will renounce this contemplative [life] . . . I

will attempt some uncommon, unexpected enterprise in law; let me lay the plan, and arouse spirit enough to push boldly. I swear I will push myself into business; I'll watch my opportunity to speak in court, and will strike with surprise—surprise bench, bar, jury, auditors and all. Activity, boldness, forwardness, will draw attention.... I will not confine myself to a chamber for nothing. I'll have some boon in return, exchange: fame, fortune, or something.... I'd rather be lost in a whirlwind of activity, study, business, great and good designs of promoting the honor, grandeur, wealth, happiness of mankind.[5]

> His diary could also be severe on manners as well as character, as in talking about a conversation with Rev. William Smith of Weymouth (who would become his father-in-law).

I talked to Parson Smith about despising gay dress, grand buildings and estates, fame, etc., and being contented with what will satisfy the real wants of nature. All this is affectation and ostentation.... Besides this, I have insensibly fallen into a habit of affecting wit and humor; of shrugging my shoulders, and moving and distorting the muscles of my face. My motions are stiff and uneasy, ungraceful; and my attention is unsteady and irregular.[6]

> Nevertheless, Adams was making his way in the world and, at twenty-five, by design or necessity, entered public service as Braintree's surveyor of highways.

In March, when I had no suspicion, I heard my name pronounced in a nomination of surveyors of highways. I was very wroth, because I knew no better, but said nothing. My friend, Dr. [Elisha] Savil, came to me and told me that he had nominated me, to prevent me from being nominated as a constable. "For," said the Doctor, "they make it a rule to compel every man to serve either as constable or surveyor, or to pay a fine." I said, "they might as well have chosen any boy in school, for I knew nothing of the business; but since they had chosen me at a venture, I would accept it in the same manner, and find out my duty as I could."

> Lack of experience no obstacle, Adams threw himself into building a highway bridge—"ploughing, ditching, blowing rocks upon Penn's Hill, and building an entire new bridge of stone—"

The best workmen in town were employed in laying the foundation and placing the bridge, but the next spring brought down a flood that threw my bridge all into ruins. The materials remained, and were afterwards relaid in a more durable manner; and the blame fell upon the workmen, not upon me. For all agreed that I had executed my office with impartiality, diligence, and spirit.[7]

> His reputation as highway surveyor profited from persistence in building bridges. His next crusade foreshadowed the future as passion for principle proved to be poor politics.

I was fired with a zeal, amounting to enthusiasm, against ardent spirits, the multiplication of taverns, retailers, and dram-shops, and tippling houses. Grieved to the heart to see the number of idlers, thieves, sots, and consumptive patients made for the physicians in those infamous seminaries, I applied to the Court of Sessions, procured a committee of inspection and inquiry, reduced the number of licensed houses, etc. But I only acquired the reputation of a hypocrite and an ambitious demagogue by it. The number of licensed houses was soon reinstated; drams, grog, and sotting were not diminished, and remain to this day as deplorable as ever.[8]

Practicing Law

Despite this early lesson in understanding the public, Adams would preach and practice as if the function of government was to compensate for flaws in human nature—"Alas, poor human nature!"[9] When Britain began to enforce laws against smuggling, he evaded friend Jonathan Sewall's call to resist with the excuse that he lacked talent, though what he lacked was sufficient commitment.

In 1759, rumors were everywhere spread, that the English would now new-model the Colonies, demolish the charters, and reduce all to royal governments. These rumors I had heard as often as he [Sewall] had. One morning I met him accidentally on the floor of the old town-house. "John," said he, "I want to speak with you." He always called me John, and I him Jonathan; and I often said to him, I wish my name were David.

He took me to a window-seat and said, "These Englishmen are going to play the devil with us. They will overturn every thing. We must resist them, and that by force. I wish you would write in the newspapers, and urge a general attention to the militia, to their exercises and discipline, for we must resist in arms."

I answered, "All this, I fear, is true; but why do you not write yourself? You are older than I am, have more experience than I have, are more intimate with the grandees than I am, and you can write ten times better than I can."[10]

Sewall declined, too, but in February 1761, their older friend James Otis Jr. protested in court that Writs of Assistance (used to search for smuggled goods) violated legal precedent, traditional practice, and the rights of British citizens, even those in America. The scene lay inscribed indelibly in Adams's mind.

You must paint all the Boston Bar sitting at the tables

in gowns, bands, and wiggs: and even I have an ambition of a seat at that table, looking like a short, thick Archbishop of Canterbury, with a pen in my hand carelessly noting . . . miserable minutes. Would not Copley have made a great painting of that counsel chamber and its contents? . . . Mr. Gridley was engaged [on] one side of the Crown and supported his cause with his usual learning, ingenuity and dignity. . . . But Otis was a flaming fire. With a promptitude of classical allusions, a depth of research, a profusion of legal authorities, a prophetic glance of his eyes into futurity, and a torrent of impetuous overbearing eloquence, he carried all before him. The seeds of independence were sown.[11]

> So immersed in the eloquence that he forgot to take notes, Adams emerged dedicated to the Glorious Cause of freedom from Parliament's injustice.

I was much more attentive to the information and the eloquence of the speaker than to my minutes, and too much alarmed at the prospect that was opened before me to care much about writing a report of the controversy. . . . A contest appeared to me to be opened, to which I could foresee no end, and which would render my life a burden, and property, industry, and every thing insecure.[12]

> Not yet secure enough to marry, Adams nevertheless had marriage on his mind. He visited Josiah Quincy's home often, talking with Hannah Quincy, who was "always thinking or reading" and enjoyed flirting with him. Naive, not knowing whether to take her seriously, he would replay the repartee in his diary.

Wednesday, 3 January 1759.
    H.Q. Suppose you were in your study, engaged in the investigation of some point of law or philosophy, and your wife should interrupt you accidentally, and break the thread

Practicing Law

of your thoughts so that you never could recover it? . . . Should you like to spend your evenings at home in reading and conversation with your wife, rather than abroad in some taverns or with other company?

[J.A.] Should prefer the company of an agreeable wife to any other company, for the most part, not always; I should not like to be imprisoned at home. . . .

H.Q. How shall a pair avoid falling into a passion or out of humor upon some occasions, and treating each other unkindly?

[J.A.] By resolving against it. . . . But if it happens that both get out of humor and an angry dispute ensues, yet both will be sorry when their anger subsides, and mutually forgive and ask forgiveness, and love each other the better for it for the future.[13]

> Such rational discourse seduced him to the brink of an impetuous proposal. Rescued by his best friend Jonathan Sewall and Hannah's sister Esther, Adams rebounded, fortified to follow Gridley's advice against marrying young.

Sewall and Esther broke in upon Hannah and me, and interrupted a conversation that would have terminated in a courtship, which would have terminated in a marriage, which marriage might have depressed me to absolute poverty and obscurity, to the end of my life; but that accident separated us, and gave room for [Bela Lincoln's] addresses, which have delivered me from very dangerous shackles, and left me at liberty, if I will but mind my studies, of making a character and a fortune.[14]

> Within a year, he saw Hannah Quincy safely wed to Bela Lincoln, whose continual emotional abuse—even in public—wore her down. Adams, feeling responsible or

not, grimly watched her suffer grief, shame, resentment, and, ultimately, contempt—adding further weight to Gridley's warning against marriage. Hannah, more sanguine, vainly tried sparking romance between Adams and the middle daughter of Parson Smith of Weymouth,[15] Abigail Smith—who in a few years would reshape Adams's living as Otis had reshaped his thinking.

On the 25th of May [1761] my venerable father died, in his seventy-first year.... Nothing that I can say or do, can sufficiently express my gratitude for his parental kindness to me, or the exalted opinion I have of his wisdom and virtue. It was a melancholy house. My father and mother were seized at the same time with the violent fever, a kind of influenza or an epidemic, which carried off seventeen aged people in our neighborhood. My mother remained ill in bed at my father's funeral; but, being younger than my father, and possessed of a stronger constitution, she happily recovered, and lived, to my inexpressible comfort, till the year 1797, when she died at almost ninety years of age.[16] ... By his will [my father] left me a house and barn and forty acres of land, besides one third of his personal estate.[17]

> Now realizing his childhood ambition, Adams threw himself into farming with the same passionate persistence that he was applying to law and public service.

Sunday, 24 October 1762. My thoughts are running continually from the orchard to the pasture, and from thence to the swamp, and thence to the house and barn and land adjoining. Sometimes I am at the orchard ploughing up acre after acre, planting, pruning apple-trees, mending fences, carting dung; sometimes in the pasture, digging stones, clearing bushes, pruning trees, building wall to redeem posts and rails; and sometimes removing button trees

Practicing Law

down to my house; sometimes I am at the old swamp, burning bushes, digging stumps and roots, cutting ditches across the meadows against my uncle's [property] and am sometimes at the other end of the town buying posts and rails to fence against my uncle's, and against the brook; and am sometimes ploughing the upland with six yoke of oxen, and planting corn, potatoes, etc., and digging up the meadows and sowing onions, planting cabbages, etc. etc. Sometimes I am at the homestead, running cross fences, and planting potatoes by the acre, and corn by the two acres, and running a ditch along the [property] line.... Sometimes am carting gravel from the neighboring hills, and sometimes dust from the streets upon the fresh meadows, and am sometimes ploughing, sometimes digging those meadows to introduce clover and other English grasses.[18]

> A fully occupied, vigorous twenty-seven-year-old still suffering sexual tension from Hannah Quincy's teasing, bachelor Adams made a virtue of resisting temptations of the flesh.

Here it may be proper to recollect something which makes an article of great importance in the life of every man. I was of an amorous disposition, and, very early, from ten or eleven years of age, was very fond of the society of females. I had my favorites among young women, and spent many of my evenings in their company; and this disposition, although controlled for seven years after my entrance into college, returned and engaged me too much till I was married.

I shall draw no characters, nor give any enumeration of my youthful flames. It would be considered as no compliment to the dead or the living. This, I will say: they were all modest and virtuous girls, and always maintained their character through life. No virgin or matron ever had cause to blush at the sight of me, or to regret her acquaintance with me. No father, brother, son, or friend, ever had cause of grief or resentment for any intercourse between me and any daughter, sister, mother, or any other relation of the female sex. These reflections, to me congratulatory beyond all expression, I am able to make with truth and sincerity; and I presume I am indebted for this blessing to my education.[19]

> They first met when Abigail Smith was fifteen. Dark-eyed, slender, she stood about five feet seven inches. He claimed to be five seven or five nine.[20] At first she lacked Hannah Quincy's "fondness or tenderness,"[21] perhaps because she did not stimulate "that capricious, inconsiderate, wild, mad passion of Love, which never looks forward to Posterity."[22] After a few years of courtship, her rational passion matched his own. He recorded the event cooly.

I passed the summer of 1764 in attending courts and pursuing my studies, with some amusement on my little farm, to which I was frequently making additions, until the fall, when, on the 25th of October, I was married to Miss Smith, second daughter of the Rev. William Smith, granddaughter of the Honorable John Quincy of Braintree—a connection which has been the source of all my felicity.[23]

> From their marriage at ages twenty-nine and nineteen, the passion would endure nearly fifty years. The farm at Braintree functioned as the pivot in a pair of compasses—Abigail Adams the fixed foot leaning after him while John Adams whirled round the world. Southward past the hill, beyond the house lay "a wide range of bays, islands and channels seaward, with seats and villages on the intervening land."[24] As if they were the new Adam and Eve, the world lay all before them.

3

BECOMING A RADICAL

1764–1770

Their first ten years together, Abigail and John Adams lived a normal wedded life. She would have a baby almost every two years—only four surviving infancy—John Quincy, Abigail ("Abby"), Charles, and Thomas.[1] They focused John Adams's purpose to succeed as a lawyer. With the kitchen as his law office, Adams made up for what he lacked in intellect, influence, and confidence with industry and perseverance. He would gain both competence and influence in Jeremiah Gridley's junto.

1765. January 24. Thursday. Soon after I got to Boston, at January Court [Samuel] Fitch came to me, upon 'Change, and told me that Mr. Gridley and he had something to communicate to me that I should like—in sacred confidence, however. I waited on Mr. Gridley at his office (after many conjectures what the secret might be) and he told me that he and Mr. Fitch had proposed a law club, a private association for the study of law and oratory.... He was considering who was, for the future, to support the honor and dignity of the bar; and he was determined to bring me into practice, the first practice, and Fitch too.... And he was very desirous of forming a junto, a small sodality of himself and Fitch and me . . . in order to read in concert the Feudal Law and Tully's Orations. . . .

Gridley. Our plan must be, when we have finished the Feudal Law, to read Coke-Littleton, and after him a reign and the statutes of that reign. It should also be a part of our plan to improve ourselves in writing, by reading carefully the best English writers, and by using ourselves to writing. For it should be part of our plan to publish pieces now and then.[2]

> The junto deepened Adams's interest in legal history, gave guided practice in oratory, and encouraged his writing. Adams had already revealed a passion for publishing essays in the press with a semicomical series on agriculture by "Humphrey Ploughjogger" in the *Boston Gazette* (June 1763). Two years later, essays for the junto ("Dissertation on the Canon and Feudal Law") appeared anonymously in the same columns. Still unsure of himself, he deleted from the published version this idealistic vision:

I always consider the settlement of America with reverence and wonder, as the opening of a grand scene and design in Providence for the illumination of the ignorant, and the emancipation of the slavish part of mankind all over the earth.[3]

> Parliament passed the Stamp Act taxing all printed papers—including legal forms. Position papers that Adams wrote for the legislature argued from legal history that the Act was unconstitutional. Though flattered by their popularity, he worried about their effect on the public temper.

My draught was produced, and unanimously adopted without amendment, reported to the town, and accepted without a dissenting voice. These were published in [Rich-

Becoming a Radical

ard] Draper's paper [*Massachusetts Gazette*, 10 October 1765], as that printer first applied to me for a copy. They were decided and spirited enough. They rang through the State and were adopted in so many words, as I was informed by the representatives of that year, by forty towns, as instructions to their representatives. They were honored sufficiently, by the friends of government, with the epithets of inflammatory, etc. . . . They met with such strong feelings in the readers, that their effect was astonishing to me, and excited some serious reflections. I thought a man ought to be very cautious what kinds of fuel he throws into a fire, when it is thus glowing in the community.[4]

> The Boston mob needed little spark to explode. On 26 August they torched the home of stamp master Andrew Oliver and threatened his brother-in-law, Lieutenant Governor Thomas Hutchinson, wrongly suspected of hatching the stamp act.[5] Adams perceived Hutchinson as ruling an evil political empire of his own making.

An unextinguishable ambition and avarice that were ever seen among his other qualities and which grew with his growth and strengthened with his age and experience and at last predominated over every other passion of his heart and principle of his mind, rendered him credulous to a childish degree of everything that favored his ruling passion, and blind and deaf to everything that thwarted it.[6]

> Hutchinson called Adams hypersensitive to "any real or supposed personal neglect or injury" and suspicious of anyone with "more wealth, more honours, or more knowledge than himself."[7] But now Adams had to weigh anarchy in the streets against the tyranny of Hutchinson.

Wednesday, 15 August 1765. If there is no proof at all of any injury done to the people by [Oliver], has not the blind, undistinguishing rage of the rabble done him irreparable injustice? ... To be carried through the town in such insolent triumph, and burned on a hill, to have his garden torn in pieces, his house broken open, his furniture destroyed, and his whole family thrown into confusion and terror, is a very atrocious violation of the peace, and of dangerous tendency and consequence. But, on the other hand, ... has not his Honor the Lieutenant-Governor [Hutchinson] discovered to the people, in innumerable instances, a very ambitious and avaricious disposition? Has he not grasped four of the most important offices in the Province into his own hands? ... Is not this amazing ascendancy of one family foundation sufficient on which to erect a tyranny? Is it not enough to excite jealousies among the people?[8]

> With the Stamp Act in force, the courts closed. Boston appointed Adams's heroes Gridley and Otis along with Adams himself as counsels to petition reopening the courts. Again, Adams worried about what the honor could mean.

The reasons which induced Boston to choose me, at a distance and unknown as I am, the particular persons concerned and measures concerted to bring this about, I am wholly at a loss to conjecture; as I am, what the future effects [of the Stamp Act] will be both with regard to myself and the public.[9] So sudden an interruption in my career is very unfortunate for me.... Thirty years of my life are passed in preparation for business; I have had poverty to struggle with, envy and jealousy and malice of enemies to encounter, no friends, or but few, to assist me; so that I have groped in dark obscurity, till of late, and had but just become known and gained a small degree of reputation, when this execrable project [the Stamp Act] was set on foot for my ruin as well as that of America in general, and of Great Britain.[10]

Becoming a Radical

The petition came to nothing. At Boston's Monday Night Club of leading politicians he was persuaded to campaign for the Braintree board of supervisors against an alleged supporter of the Stamp Act. Adams rationalized that he won election as the lesser of two evils.

> *Monday, 3 March 1766.* I own it gave me much pleasure to find I had so many friends, and that my conduct in town has been not disapproved. The choice was quite unexpected to me. . . .The [opposition's] favorite was dropped, and I, more obnoxious to that party than . . . any other man, was chosen.[11]

Adams took the office seriously, worrying about schools, welfare, assessments, and roads. With the Stamp Act limiting his law practice, he turned to writing as avocation and even to farming for recreation—"lopping and trimming the walnuts and oaks, and felling the pines and savins and hemlocks. . . ."[12] Alas, after all his efforts, when repeal finally came and Boston erupted in rejoicing—parades, grand illuminations all over town, bonfires, skyrockets[13] —he missed the celebration.

> *Monday, 26 May 1766.* A duller day than last Monday, when the Province was in a rapture for the repeal of the Stamp Act, I do not remember to have passed. My wife, who had long depended on going to Boston, and my little babe, were both very ill of an whooping cough. Myself under obligation to attend the superior court at Plymouth the next day, and therefore unable to go to Boston, and the town of Braintree insensible to the common joy![14]

With both his practice and his family expanding—baby John Quincy now almost one—Adams overcame his reluctance to leave provincial but salubrious Braintree.

In the beginning of the year 1768, my friends in Boston were very urgent with me to remove into town. I was afraid of my health; but they urged so many reasons, and insisted on it so much, that, determined at last to hazard the experiment, I . . . removed in a week or two with my family into the White House, as it was called, in Brattle Square.[15]

> With the added expense of living in Boston, Adams could have compromised principles for profit and for power as an official under Lieutenant Governor Hutchinson.

In the course of this year, 1768, my friend, Mr. Jonathan Sewall, who was then Attorney-General, called on me, in Brattle Street, and told me he was come to dine with me. This was always an acceptable favor from him; for although we were at antipodes in politics, we had never abated in mutual esteem, or cooled in the warmth of our friendship. After dinner, Mr. Sewall desired to have some conversation with me alone, and proposed adjourning to the office. Mrs. Adams arose, and chose to adjourn to her chamber. We were accordingly left alone. Mr. Sewall then said he waited on me, at that time, at the request of the Governor, Mr. [Francis] Bernard, who had sent for him a few days before, and charged him with a message to me. The office of Advocate-General in the Court of Admiralty was then vacant, and the Governor . . . would write an immediate recommendation of me to his Majesty. . . .

Although this offer was unexpected to me, I was in an instant prepared for an answer. The offer was lucrative in itself, and a sure introduction to the most profitable business in the Province; and what was of more consequence still, it was a first step in the ladder of royal favor and promotion. But I had long weighed this subject in my own mind. For seven years I had been solicited . . . to apply to the Governor or to the Lieutenant Governor to procure me

Becoming a Radical

a commission for the peace. [A justice of the peace] was wanted in the country, where I had lived, and it would have been of very considerable advantage to me. But I had always rejected these proposals, on account of the unsettled state of the country—the new statutes had been passed in Parliament, laying duties on glass, paint, etc. and a board of commissioners of the revenue was expected, which must excite a great fermentation in the country, of the consequences of which I could see no end—and my scruples about laying myself under any restraints or obligations of gratitude to the government for any of their favors.[16]

> Despite their potential for rabble-rousing, Adams enjoyed the homage paid to him from the Sons of Liberty, who were increasingly restive as soldiers arrived to monitor the new revenue laws.

Through the whole succeeding Fall and Winter, a regiment was exercised by Major [John] Small, in Brattle Square, directly in front of my house. The spirit-stirring drum and the ear-piercing fife aroused me and my family early enough every morning, and the indignation they excited, though somewhat soothed, was not allayed by the sweet songs, violins and flutes of the serenading Sons of Liberty under my windows in the evening. In this way and a thousand others, I had sufficient intimations that the hopes and confidence of the people were placed in me as one of their friends; and I was determined that, as far as depended on me they should not be disappointed; and that if I could render them no positive assistance, at least I would never take any part against them.

I was solicited to go to the town meetings and harangue there. This I constantly refused. My friend, Dr. [Joseph] Warren, the most frequently urged me to this. My answer to him always was, "That way madness lies."... I had learned enough to show me, in all their dismal colors, the deceptions to which the people in their passions are liable, and the total suppression of equity and humanity in the human breast, when thoroughly heated and hardened by party spirit.[17]

> Nevertheless, emboldened by public support, Adams wrote the position papers for Boston's representatives during two riot-plagued crises in 1768 and 1769. He defended John Hancock against a court order for smuggling. Arguing expertly from legal history, he showed that the order from Hutchinson's court was indeed unconstitutional.

There were few days through the whole winter, when I was not summoned to attend the Court of Admiralty. It seemed as if the officers of the Crown were determined to examine the whole town as witnesses.... I was thoroughly weary of and disgusted with the court, the officers of the Crown, the cause, and even with the tyrannical bell that dangled me out of my house every morning.[18]

> In another landmark case, spring 1769, Adams defended merchant seamen charged with murdering an officer who tried to draft them into the navy. With complete confidence, Adams proved such impressment unconstitutional, doubly delighted to free the seamen and to once more defeat Hutchinson.[19]

Michael Corbett and three other Irish sailors coming in from sea on board a vessel of Mr. Hooper's of Marblehead, were sought by Lieutenant Panton and a midshipman of the *Rose* Frigate at the head of a press gang. The sailors retreated to the forepeak, and there, armed with such instruments as they could snatch in their flight, stood upon their defence. A parley ensued. Corbett said, "I know you are a lieutenant of a man-of-war, come to impress us. We are determined to defend ourselves. You have no right to force us."

Much altercation ensued. Some attempts were made to break down the bulkhead, and the midshipman in confusion fired a pistol, and wounded one of the four sailors in the arm. This the lieutenant reproved, but attempted to enter. Corbett thrust him back, and marking a line in the cargo of salt in the hold, said, "If you step over that mark again I shall take it as a proof of your determination to impress me, and by the eternal God of Heaven, you are a dead man."

"Ay, my lad," says Panton, "I have seen a brave fellow before now"—took his snuff box out of his pocket, and snuffing up a pinch, resolutely stepped over the line. Corbett instantly threw an harpoon iron, which cut off the carotid artery and jugular vein. Panton cry'd, "The rascal has killed me," and fell dead in a few minutes. A reinforcement came to the press gang and the four men were taken. . . .[20]

I cannot say whether I ought to laugh, or cry, or scold, in reporting the trial. . . . You may easily believe I was anxious; the lives of four honest men in my hands, and a sympathizing world looking to me for exertions to preserve them. . . . I presented and read my pleas. No counsel for the Crown ordered to answer these pleas, not a word said at the bar or on the bench for them or against them, when Hutchinson, not slow-rising but starting up, moved that the Court should adjourn to the council chamber. Every vote was ready, and away went their Excellencies, Honors, and learned Judges, to secret conclave. . . .

The next morning . . . it then became my turn to speak in defence of the prisoners. I had taken more pains in that case than in any other, before or since; I had appealed to Heaven and earth; I had investigated all laws, human and divine; I had searched all the authorities in the civil law, the law of nature and nations, the common law, history, practice, and every thing that could have any relation to the subject. All my books were on the table before me, and I vainly felt as if I could shake the town and the world.

A crowded audience attending, still as midnight, in eager anticipation. I had scarcely risen and said, "May it please your Excellencies and your Honors, my defence of the prisoners is, that the melancholy action for which they stand is justifiable homicide, and therefore no crime at all," and produced one authority very plump to the purpose—when Hutchinson again darted up, and moved that the Court should remove to the council chamber! No reason was given; not a word was said; the Pope's bull was implicitly and unanimously obeyed, and away marched their Excellencies and Honors to the council chamber....

Never was a more gloomy assembly of countenances painted with terror and horror, than appeared in the audience next morning. The Court appeared; the prisoners were ordered to the bar. The President arose, and pronounced the unanimous sentence of the court—that the killing of Lieutenant Panton was justifiable homicide in necessary self-defence...."The judgment of the Court is unanimous," and not another word was said....

There is a secret behind, that has never been hinted in public, and that Hutchinson dreaded should be produced before the public.... I had imported from London, and then possessed, the only complete set of the British Statutes at Large that then existed in Boston and, as I believe, in all the Colonies. In that work is a statute which expressly prohibits impressments in America.

> (The statute of 1707, to encourage transatlantic trade, outlawed impressing seamen "imployed in any part of America."[21])

Becoming a Radical

The volume which contains that statute, doubled down in dog's ears, I had before me, on the table, with a heap of other books. I was determined that if the law of God, of nature, of nations, of the common law of England, and our American prescriptions and charters, could not preserve the lives of my clients, that statute should, if it could. The conclave dreaded the publication of that statute, which they intended to get repealed, and which they and their successors have since procured to be repealed.[22]

> Swept up by popularity, Adams accepted a seat in the legislature. Abigail Adams, losing their baby Susanna and pregnant with Charles, had to pack up and move to a new house while public unrest roiled through Boston streets.

When I went home to my family in May 1770, from the town meeting in Boston ... where I had been chosen in my absence, without any solicitation, one of their representatives, I said to my wife, "I have accepted a seat in the House of Representatives, and thereby have consented to my own ruin, to your ruin, and the ruin of our children. I give you this warning that you may prepare your mind for your fate." She burst into tears, but instantly cried out in a transport of magnanimity, "Well I am willing in this cause to run all risks with you and to be ruined with you if you are ruined." These were times ... which tried women's souls as well as men's.[23]

> Troops quartered on unwilling citizens and underpaid, competing with citizens for menial jobs and women, fired on a threatening mob of about a dozen, killing five. In defending them, Adams confronted a more ominous crisis.

The evening of the fifth of March I spent ... at the south end of Boston, in company with a club with whom I had been associated for several years. About nine o'clock we were alarmed with the ringing of bells, and supposing it to be the signal of fire, we snatched our hats and cloaks.... In the street we were informed that the British soldiers had fired on the inhabitants, killed some and wounded others, near the town-house. A crowd of people was flowing down the street to the scene of action. When we arrived, we saw nothing but some field-pieces placed before the south door of the town-house, and some engineers and grenadiers drawn up to protect them.

Mrs. Adams was then in circumstances [about eight months pregnant with Charles] to make me apprehensive of the effect of the surprise upon her, who was alone, excepting her maids and a boy, in the house. Having therefore surveyed round the town-house, and seeing all quiet, I ... went directly home to Cole Lane. My wife having heard that the town was still and likely to continue so, had recovered from her first apprehensions, and we had nothing but our reflections to interrupt our repose.

These reflections were to me disquieting enough. Endeavors had been systematically pursued for many months, by certain busy characters, to excite quarrels, rencounters, and combats, single or compound, in the night, between the inhabitants of the lower class and the soldiers, and at all risks to enkindle an immortal hatred between them. I suspected that this was the explosion which had been intentionally wrought up by designing men, who knew what they were aiming at better than the instruments employed. If these poor tools should be prosecuted for any of their illegal conduct, they must be punished. If the soldiers in self-defense should kill any of them, they must be tried, and, if truth were respected and the law prevailed, must be acquitted. To depend upon the perversion of the law, and the

Becoming a Radical

corruption or partiality of juries, would insensibly disgrace the jurisprudence of the country and corrupt the morals of the people.... These were my meditations in the night.

The next morning, I think it was, sitting in my office, near the steps of the town-house stairs, Mr. [James] Forrest came in.... With tears streaming from his eyes, he said, "I am come with a very solemn message from a very unfortunate man, Captain [Thomas] Preston, in prison.... I had no hesitation in answering... he must be sensible this would be as important a cause as was ever tried in any court or country of the world.... He must expect from me no art or address, no sophistry or prevarication, in such a cause, nor any thing more than fact, evidence, and law would justify.

"Captain Preston," he said, "would require no more; and that he had had such an opinion from all he had heard from all parties of me, that he could cheerfully trust his life with me...."[24]

My sense of equity and humanity impelled me, against a torrent of unpopularity and the inclination of all my friends....[25] It was immediately bruited abroad that I had engaged for Preston and the soldiers, and occasioned a great clamor, which the friends of government were delighted to hear, and slily and secretly fomented with all their art.[26]

> Adams, feeling himself about to be victimized by circumstances, once more relied on Abigail Adams, with troubles of her own, to share the pain, heal the hurt, soothe the spirit.

At this time I had more business at the bar than any man in the Province. My health was feeble. I was throwing away as bright prospects as any man ever had before him, and I had devoted myself to endless labor and anxiety, if not to infamy and to death, and that for nothing, except what indeed was and ought to be all in all, a sense of duty.

In the evening, I expressed to Mrs. Adams all my apprehensions. That excellent lady, who has always encouraged me, burst into a flood of tears, but said she was very sensible of all the danger to her and to our children, as well as to me, but she thought I had done as I ought; she was very willing to share in all that was to come, and to place her trust in Providence.[27]

Before or after the trial, Preston sent me ten guineas, and at the trial of the soldiers afterwards, eight guineas more, which were all the fees I ever received or were offered to me, and I should not have said any thing on the subject if they had never offered me any thing. This was all the pecuniary reward I ever had for fourteen or fifteen days labor in the most exhausting and fatiguing causes I ever tried, for hazarding a popularity very general and very hardly earned, and for incurring a clamor, popular suspicions and prejudices, which are not yet worn out, and never will be forgotten as long as the history of this period is read.[28]

4

RECONCILING IDEA AND INCLINATION

1770–1774

Adams's triumphs over Hutchinson established him as a champion of civil rights. Now he had to reconcile respect for the rule of law with a rising need for reform at a time when mob action among Boston's "motley rabble of saucy boys, negroes and molattoes, Irish teagues and outlandish jack tarrs" portended revolution.

If Heaven, in its anger, shall ever permit the time to come when, by means of an abandoned administration at home, and the outrages of the soldiery here, the bonds of parental affection and filial duty between Britain and the colonies shall be dissolved, when we shall be shaken loose from the shackles of the common law and our allegiance, and reduced to a state of nature, the American and British soldier must fight it out upon the principles of law of nature and of nations. But it is certain such a time is not yet arrived, and every virtuous Briton and American prays it never may. Till then, however, we must try causes in the tribunals of justice, by the law of the land.[1]

Adams believed defending the soldiers' rights had been,

"one of the most gallant, generous, manly, and disinterested actions of my whole life, and one of the best pieces of service I ever rendered my country."[2] It came at considerable cost. Added to research and writing, riding the court circuit, and working on many legislative committees, the trial cost him his health. He felt chest pains and shortness of breath similar to the malaise that a decade earlier had forced him to leave Worcester. Since then, he had acquired work habits approximating addiction that demanded withdrawal.

The complicated cares of my legal and political engagements, the slender diet to which I was obliged to confine myself, the air of the town of Boston, which was not favorable to me, who had been born and passed almost all my life in the country, but especially the constant obligation to speak in public, almost every day for many hours, had exhausted my health, brought on a pain in my breast, and a complaint in my lungs, which seriously threatened my life, and compelled me to throw off a great part of the load of business, both public and private, and return to my farm in the country.

Early in the Spring of 1771, I removed my family to Braintree, still holding, however, an office in Boston. The air of my native spot, and the fine breezes from the sea on one side, and the rocky mountains of pine and savin on the other, together with daily rides on horseback and the amusements of agriculture, always delightful to me, soon restored my health in a considerable degree.[3]

I felt a joy, I enjoyed a pleasure, in revisiting my old haunts, and recollecting my old meditations, among the rocks and trees, which was very intense indeed. The rushing torrent, the purling stream, the gurgling rivulet, the dark thicket, the rugged ledges and precipices, are all old acquain-

Reconciling Idea and Inclination

tances of mine. The young trees, walnuts and oaks, which were pruned and trimmed by me, are grown remarkably. Nay, the pines have grown the better for lopping.[4]

> Once Adams restored his spirits, he recovered his old work habits. From Braintree, he would commute to Boston in his chaise, burrowing into the office mornings by nine,[5] persevering at prosperity until the pace brought on a relapse. For rest and restoration this time he tried the Connecticut Valley.

I was advised to take a journey to the Stafford Springs, in Connecticut, then in as much vogue as any mineral springs have been in since. I spent a few days in drinking the waters, and made an excursion through Somers and Windsor down to Hartford, and the journey was of use to me, whether the waters were or not.[6]

> Adams would exclaim, "I have spent this morning in riding through paradise."[7] But enforced idleness made him feel restless, homesick, and useless.

I begin to grow weary of this idle, romantic jaunt; I believe it would have been as well to have staid in my own country and amused myself with my farm, and rode to Boston every day. I shall not suddenly take such a ramble again merely for my health. I want to see my wife, my children, my farm, my horse, oxen, cows, walls, fences, workmen, office, books, and clerks; I want to hear the news and politics of the day.... I feel guilty; I feel as if I ought not to saunter, and loiter, and trifle away this time; I feel as if I ought to be employed for the benefit of my fellow men in some way or other.[8] ... I have had a naked, barren journey; my brains have been as barren the whole time as a sandy plain or a gravelly knoll; my soul has been starved.[9]

> Upon his return, he was frustrated to find Hutchinson's

popularity rising regardless of how often Adams exposed him as an architect of "perpetual discontent."

Hutchinson, by countenancing and supporting a system of corruption and all tyranny, has made himself Governor, and by the mad idolatry of the people, always the surest instruments of their own servitude, laid prostrate at the feet of both. With great anxiety and hazard, with continual application to business, with loss of health, reputation, profit, and as fair prospects and opportunities of advancement as others who have greedily embraced them, I have, for ten years together, invariably opposed this system and its fautors [supporters]. It has prevailed, in some measure, and the people now worshipping the authors and abettors of it, and despising, insulting, and abusing the opposers of it. . . . I am, for what I can see, quite left alone in the world.[10]

> It would take two more years for Hutchinson's own letters to expose worse villainy, while Adams would sour on riding the circuit, finding it unfulfilling—"spiritless, tasteless."

I feel myself weary of this wandering life; my heart is at home. It would be more for my health to ride to Boston every fair morning, and to Braintree every fair afternoon. . . . I could then have one eye to my office, and another to my farm.[11]

> With some niggling unease about idleness, he would ramble about the farm, commute to the Boston office, and escort Abigail and Abby Adams on visits. Then with the birth of baby Thomas in September 1772, Adams began to brood about family expenses. If they were to move back to Boston it would mean an increase in business, but at the risk of reigniting his old passions for politics.

Reconciling Idea and Inclination

At thirty-seven years of age almost, this is all that my most intense application to study and business has been able to accomplish, an application that has more than once been very near costing me my life, and that has so greatly impaired my health.... I shall come with a fixed resolution to meddle not with public affairs of town or Province. I am determined my own life and the welfare of my whole family, which is much dearer to me, are too great sacrifices for me to make. I have served my country and her professed friends, at an immense expense to me of time, peace, money, and preferment.... I will devote myself wholly to my private business, my office and my farm, and I hope to lay a foundation for better fortune to my children, and a happier life than has fallen to my share.[12]

> Adams could have pleaded ill health and pressures of practice when James Otis Jr. accused him of trying to avoid civic responsibility.
>
> Says Otis to me, "You will never learn military exercises."
> "Ay, why not?"
> "That you have a head for it, needs no commentary, but not a heart."
> "Ay, how do you know? You never searched my heart."
> "Yes, I have. Tired with one year's service [in the General Court], dancing from Boston to Braintree, and from Braintree to Boston; moping about the streets of this town as hipped as Father Flynt at ninety, and seemingly regardless of every thing but to get money enough to carry you smoothly through this world."[13]
>
> Steadfast, Adams brushed off the criticism. "The storm shall blow over me in silence."[14] By the end of 1772, he had found his measure of happiness.
>
> My [stepfather], Mr. Hall, and my mother, are well

settled in my farm at Braintree. The produce of my farm is all collected in; my own family is removed and well settled in Boston; my wood and stores are laid in for the winter; my workmen are nearly all paid; I am disengaged from public affairs, and now have nothing to do but to mind my office, my clerks, and my children.[15]

1773. January the first, being Friday. I never was happier in my whole life than I have been since I returned to Boston. I feel easy and composed and contented. The year to come will be a pleasant, a cheerful, a happy, and a prosperous year to me.[16]

> This euphoria was to last only a few days. Governor Hutchinson, impatient with the drift toward Independence, proclaimed "the supreme authority of Parliament" over the provincial legislature.[17] The legislature begged Adams to write their reply.

Can I describe . . . the state of my mind at that time? I had a wife—and what a wife! I had children—and what children! . . . I knew here was nothing for me to depend on but popular breath, which I knew to be as variable and uncertain as any one of the thirty-two points of the compass. In this situation I should have thought myself the happiest man in the world, if I could have retired to my little hut and forty acres, which my father left me in Braintree, and lived on potatoes and sea-weed for the rest of my life. But I had taken a part, I had adopted a system, I had encouraged my fellow-citizens, and I could not abandon them in conscience nor in honor. I determined, therefore, to set friends and enemies at defiance, and follow my own best judgment, whatever might fall thereon . . .

> For the oratorical flourishes written by cousin Sam Adams

Reconciling Idea and Inclination

in the first draft, John Adams substituted legal and historical authorities to demolish Hutchinson's logic.

The Governor's reasoning, instead of convincing the people that Parliament had sovereign authority over them in all cases whatsoever, seemed to convince all the world that Parliament had no authority over them in any case whatsoever. . . . He had waded beyond his depth. He had wholly misunderstood the legal doctrine of allegiance.

> Although Hutchinson still could deny him a seat on the General Council, Adams mocked his ignorance.

I had quoted largely from a law authority which no man in Massachusetts, at that time, had ever read. . . . It was humorous enough to see how Hutchinson wriggled to evade it. He found nothing better to say than that it was "the artificial reasoning of Lord Coke." The book was Moore's Reports. The owner of it—for, alas! it was borrowed—was a buyer, but not a reader, of books. It had been Mr. Gridley's.[18]

> Loins thus girded, Adams had returned to the lists. He gloried in the challenge.

I have never known a period in which the seeds of great events have been so plentifully sown as this winter [of 1773–74]. A Providence is visible in that concurrence of causes, which produced the debates and controversies of this winter. The Court of Inquisition at Rhode Island [on the sinking of the revenue cutter, Gaspée, with the threat of sending any accused to Britain for trial], the Judges' [independence from the governor], the Massachusetts Bay town meetings, General William Brattle's folly [in wishing to debate him on independence of judges] all conspired in a remarkable, a wonderful manner. My own determination had been to decline all invitations to public affairs and inquiries. But

Brattle's rude, indecent, and unmeaning challenge, of me in particular, laid me under peculiar obligations to undeceive the people, and changed my resolution.[19]

> He wrote six weekly pieces for the *Boston Gazette,* making Brattle look ridiculous. But remembering Stamp Act riots, Adams feared Hutchinson's revoking independence of judges would trigger more violence.

At this period, the universal cry among the friends of their country was, "What shall we do to be saved?" It was by all agreed, as the Governor was entirely dependent on the Crown, and the Council in danger of becoming so, if the judges were made so too, the liberties of the country would be totally lost, and every man at the mercy of a few slaves of the Governor.... Some of these judges were men of resolution, and the Chief Justice [Peter Oliver] ... had so often gloried in it on the bench, that I shuddered at the expectation that the mob might put on him a coat of tar and feathers, if not put him to death. ... I dreaded the effect upon the morals and tempers of the people, which must be produced by any violence offered to the persons of those who wore the robes and bore the sacred characters of judges; and moreover, I felt a strong aversion to such partial and irregular recurrences to original power.

> Once more, Adams found refuge in authorities and precedents. He could justify the impeachment of Hutchinson's judges as illegally appointed.

I believed there was one constitutional resource.... Several voices at once cried out, "A constitutional resource! what can it be?" I said it was nothing more nor less than an impeachment of the Judges, by the House of Representatives, before the Council.
"An impeachment! why, such a thing is without precedent."

Reconciling Idea and Inclination

I believed it was, in this Province; but there had been precedents enough, and by much too many, in England; it was a dangerous experiment at all times, but it was essential to the preservation of the constitution in some cases that could be reached by no other power. . . . It soon became the common topic and research of the bar.[20]

As jurors refused to serve judges under indictment, Adams foiled Hutchinson once more. The Boston Tea Party, however, created new issues. He called it, "The grandest event which has ever yet happened since the controversy with Britain opened. The sublimity of it charms me!"[21] Yet his diary reflected the ongoing conflict between traditional rule of law and expediency of political action.

This destruction of the tea is so bold, so daring, so firm, intrepid and inflexible, and it must have so important consequences, and so lasting, that I cannot but consider it as an epocha in history. This, however, is but an attack upon property. Another similar exertion of populist power may produce the destruction of lives. . . . To let [the tea] be landed would be . . . losing all our labor for ten years, and subjecting ourselves and our posterity forever to Egyptian taskmasters; to burthens, indignities; to ignominy, reproach and contempt; to desolation and oppression; to poverty and servitude.[22]

When defending Maine merchant Richard King, who for ten years was a victim of mobs as a suspected Tory, Adams tried to distinguish between lawful and unlawful political activity.

These private mobs I do and will detest. If popular commotions can be justified in opposition to attacks upon the Constitution, it can be only when fundamentals are invaded, nor then unless for absolute necessity, and with great caution.

But these tarrings and featherings, this breaking open houses by rude and insolent rabble in resentment for private wrongs, or in pursuance of private prejudices and passions, must be discountenanced.[23]

> In this spirit, Adams chaired a town meeting to protest closing Boston's port. He packed the family off to Braintree before touring the circuit one last time. He could not insulate himself from the troubles ahead. He had a fatal flaw in the zeal he could not hide.

I cannot avoid exposing myself . . . my feelings will at all times overcome my modesty and reserve, my prudence, policy, and discretion. I have a zeal at my heart for my country and her friends, which I cannot smother or conceal; it will burn out at times and in companies where it ought to be latent in my breast. This zeal will prove fatal to the fortune and felicity of my family, if it is not regulated by a cooler judgment than mine has hitherto been.[24]

I am determined to be cool, if I can. I have suffered such torments in my mind heretofore as have almost overpowered my constitution, without any advantage. And now I will laugh and be easy if I can, let the contest of parties terminate as it will, let my own estate and interest suffer what it will, nay, whether I stand high or low in the estimation of the world, so long as I keep a conscience void of offense towards God and man.[25]

> Political encounters on the circuit helped fire his zeal. A warning from Jonathan Sewall, former best friend and now political adversary, rekindled his determination once more—as in repealing the Stamp Act—to redress grievances against Parliament.

Mr. Sewall invited me to take a walk with him, very early in the morning, on the great hill. In the course of our rambles, he very soon began to remonstrate against my going to Congress. He said that "Great Britain was determined on her system; her power was irresistible, and would certainly be destructive to me, and to all those who should persevere in opposition to her designs."

I answered, "that I knew Great Britain was determined on her system, and that very determination determined me on mine; that he knew I had been constant and uniform in opposition to all her measures; that the die was now cast; I had passed the Rubicon; swim or sink, live or die, survive or perish with my country, was my unalterable determination."[26]

At the same time, the voice of the people Adams overheard sounded ominous.

In 1774, on a journey to some of our circuit courts in Massachusetts, I stopped one night at a tavern in Shrewsbury, about forty miles from Boston, and as I was cold and wet, I sat down at a good fire in the bar-room to dry my great coat and saddle-bags till a fire could be made in my chamber. There presently came in, one after another, half a dozen, or half a score, substantial yeomen of the neighborhood, who, sitting down to the fire after lighting their pipes, began a lively conversation upon politics. As I believed I was unknown to all of them, I sat in total silence to hear them.

One said, "The people of Boston are distracted!" Another answered, "No wonder the people of Boston are distracted. Oppression will make wise men mad."

A third said, "What would you say, if a fellow should come to your house and tell you he was come to make a list of your cattle, that parliament might tax you for them at so much a head? And how should you feel, if he was to go and break open your barn, to take down your oxen, cows, horses, and sheep?"

"What should I say?" replied the first; "I would knock him in the head."

"Well," said a fourth, "if parliament can take away Mr. Hancock's wharf and Mr. Rowe's wharf, they can take away your barn and my house."

After much more reasoning in this style, a fifth, who had as yet been silent, broke out, "Well, it is high time for us to rebel...." I was disgusted with his word *rebel*, because I was determined never to rebel, as much as I was to resist rebellion against the fundamental privileges of the Constitution.[27]

> That summer he wrote to Abigail Adams almost daily—even from Boston—revealing a conflict between love and duty: homesick at heart, unsettled in mind, yet engaged for the first Continental Congress in September.

I believe it is time to think a little about my family and farm. The fine weather we have had for eight or ten days past I hope has been carefully improved to get in my hay. It is a great mortification to me that I could not attend every step of their progress in mowing, making, and carting. I long to see what burden. But I long more still to see to the procuring more sea-weed, and muscle mud, and sand, etc.

However, my prospect is interrupted again. I shall have no time. I must prepare for a journey to Philadelphia, a long journey indeed! But if the length of the journey were all, it would be no burden. But the consideration of what is to be done is of great weight. Great things are wanted to be done, and little things only I fear can be done. I dread the thought of the Congress' falling short of the expectations of the continent, but especially of the people of this province.

Vapors avaunt! I will do my duty, and leave the event. If

Reconciling Idea and Inclination

I have the approbation of my own mind, whether applauded or censured, blessed or cursed, by the world, I will not be unhappy.

Certainly I shall enjoy good company, good conversation, and shall have a fine ride and see a little more of the world than I have seen before.

> Amid talk of linens that would withstand washing and whether to have a new suit made in Boston or Philadelphia came an ominous reminder to Abigail Adams.

The letters I have written, or may write, my dear, must be kept secret, or at least shown with great caution.[28]

> To self-doubt Adams now added doubt about the competence of fellow delegates to the Congress.

Monday, 20 June 1774. There is a new and a grand scene open before me; a Congress. This will be an assembly of the wisest men upon the continent, who are Americans in principle, that is, against the taxation of Americans by authority of Parliament. I feel myself unequal to this business. A more extensive knowledge of the realm, the colonies, and of commerce, as well as of law and policy, is necessary, than I am master of.

Saturday, 25 June 1774. I have taken a long walk through ... a fine tract of land in a general field. Corn, rye, grass, interspersed in great perfection this fine season. I wander alone and ponder. I muse, I mope, I ruminate. I am often in reveries and brown studies. The objects before me are too grand and multifarious for my comprehension. We have not men fit for the times. We are deficient in genius, in education, in travel, in fortune, in every thing—I feel unutterable anxiety.—God grant us wisdom and fortitude! Should the opposition be suppressed, should this country submit, what infamy and ruin! God forbid. Death in any form is less terrible!²⁹

5

MANEUVERING INDEPENDENCE

1774–1775

Even as Boston bid its congressional delegation a gala farewell, impatient George III was declaring, "The die is now cast, the colonies must either submit or triumph."[1] John Adams, along with Sam Adams, Thomas Cushing, and Robert Treat Paine, still enjoyed cordial ceremonies on the way to Philadelphia. In the course of two congresses there, Adams would suffer anxiety, inactivity, and impatience in silence until Britain's brutality in Massachusetts and John Dickinson's arrogant obstructions in Congress inflamed his zeal to write, speak, and intrigue for open rebellion. At first, however, he enjoyed Philadelphia's hospitality freely.

Wednesday, 7 September 1774. Dined with Mr. Miers Fisher a young Quaker and a lawyer. We saw his library, which is clever. But this plain Friend and his plain though pretty wife, with her Thees and Thous, had provided us the most costly entertainment; ducks, hams, chickens, beef, pig, tarts, creams, custards, jellies, fools, trifles, floating islands, beer, porter, punch, wine, and a long etc.

Thursday, 8 September 1774. Dined at Mr. [Samuel] Powel's ... a most sinful feast again! every thing which could delight the eye or allure the taste; curds and creams, jellies, sweetmeats of various sorts, twenty sorts of tarts . . . whipped syllabubs [custards], etc. etc., Parmesan cheese, punch, wine, porter, beer, etc.²

> At the same time, Adams's imagination feasted upon a warning to be wary from local Sons of Liberty.

"Now," said they, "you must not utter the word 'independence,' nor give the least hint or insinuation of the idea, either in Congress or any private conversation; if you do, you are undone; for the idea of independence is as unpopular in Pennsylvania, and in all the Middle and Southern States, as the Stamp Act itself. No man dares to speak of it. . . .

"You are thought to be too warm, too zealous, too sanguine. You must be, therefore, very cautious; you must not come forward with any bold measures, you must not pretend to take the lead. . . . [Virginians] think they have a right to take the lead, and the Southern States, and Middle States too, are too much disposed to yield it to them. . . ."

It soon became rumored about the city that John Adams was for independence. The Quakers and proprietary gentlemen took the alarm; represented me as the worst of men; the true-blue sons of liberty pitied me; all put me under a kind of coventry. I was avoided, like a man infected with the leprosy. I walked the streets of Philadelphia in solitude, borne down by the weight of care and unpopularity.³

> Adams's moods swung from conviviality and delusions of being despised, to real anxiety, then cautious optimism as rumors reporting a British attack on Boston proved false.

We are waiting with the utmost anxiety and impatience for further intelligence. The effect of the news we have, both upon Congress and the inhabitants of this city, was very

Maneuvering Independence

great. Great indeed! Every gentleman seems to consider the bombardment of Boston as the bombardment of the capital of his own province.[4]

When the horrid news was brought here of the bombardment of Boston, which made us completely miserable for two days, we saw proofs both of the sympathy and the resolution of the continent.

War! war! war! was the cry, and it was pronounced in a tone which would have done honor to the oratory of a Briton or a Roman.

If it had proved true, you would have heard the thunder of an American Congress.[5]

When we first came together, I found a strong jealousy of us from New England, and the Massachusetts in particular; suspicions entertained of designs of independency; an American republic; Presbyterian principles, and twenty other things. Our sentiments were heard in Congress with great caution, and seemed to make but little impression; but the longer we sat, the more clearly they saw the necessity of pushing vigorous measures.[6]

> Adams's optimism took a quantum leap when the Congress gave unanimous support to the Suffolk Resolves for restoring "just rights," harmony, and union with Great Britain.[7]

Saturday, 17 September 1774. This was one of happiest days of my life. In Congress we had generous, noble sentiments, and manly eloquence. This day convinced me that America will support the Massachusetts or perish with her.[8]

The fixed determination that [the Resolves] should be supported, were enough to melt a heart of stone. I saw the tears gush into the eyes of the old grave pacific Quakers of Pennsylvania.[9]

> Adams probably appeared quiescent, but he grew more and more impatient as debaters tediously nitpicked petitions and addresses to the throne.

[25 September 1774] Tedious indeed is our business—slow as snails. I have not been used to such ways... Fifty gentlemen meeting together, all strangers, are not acquainted with each other's language, ideas, views, designs. They are therefore jealous of each other—fearful, timid, skittish....

[29 September 1774] We go to Congress at nine, and there we stay, most earnestly engaged in debates upon the most abstruse mysteries of state, until three in the afternoon; then we adjourn, and go to dine with some of the nobles of Pennsylvania at four o'clock, and feast upon ten thousand delicacies, and sit drinking Madeira, Claret, and Burgundy, till six or seven, and then go home fatigued to death with business, company, and care....

[9 October 1774] I am wearied to death with the life I lead. The business of the Congress is tedious beyond expression. This assembly is like no other that ever existed. Every man in it is a great man, an orator, a critic, a statesman; and therefore every man upon every question must show his oratory, his criticism, and his political abilities.... I believe if it was moved and seconded that we should come to a resolution that three and two make five, we should be entertained with logic and rhetoric, law, history, politics, and mathematics, and then—we should pass the resolution unanimously in the affirmative.[10]

> Persevering, Adams served on four committees. He wrote private letters, character sketches of delegates, many notes on the secret debates, and drafts of position papers. As the

Maneuvering Independence

first Congress closed, he left Philadelphia in a heavy rain that contrasted with the brightness in his heart on going home.

[26 October 1774] This day the Congress finished. Spent the evening together at the City Tavern; all the Congress, and several gentlemen of the town.

[28 October 1774] Took our departure, in a very great rain. . . . It is not very likely that I shall ever see this part of the world again.[11]

> Adams returned home to find that besides Boston's port, the British had closed legislature, council, and courts. He said that he preferred a peaceful resolution.

I have bent my chief attention to prevent a rupture, and to impress my friends with the importance of preventing it. . . . The death of four or five persons, the most obscure and inconsiderable that could have been found upon the continent, on the 5th of March 1770, has never yet been forgiven by any part of America. What, then, would be the consequence of a battle in which many thousands must fall, of the best blood, the best families, fortunes, abilities, and moral characters in the country?[12]

> Yet, from January to mid-April of 1775 he published a dozen polemical essays as by "Novanglus" in the *Boston Gazette* warning that patriots stood ready to resist tyranny with arms. The series was cut off when, he said, "The battle of Lexington, on the 19th of April, changed the instruments of warfare from the pen to the sword."[13]

A few days after this event, I rode to Cambridge, where I saw . . . the New England army. There was great confusion and much distress. Artillery, arms, clothing were wanting, and a sufficient supply of provisions not easily obtained. Neither the officers nor men, however, wanted spirits or resolution. I rode from thence to Lexington, and along the scene of action for many miles, and inquired of the inhabitants the circumstances. These were not calculated to diminish my ardor in the cause; they, on the contrary, convinced me that the die was cast [echoing George III] ... and if we did not defend ourselves, they would kill us.[14]

> The scene must have been sickening, with crusted blood from both sides. (A British trooper alleged the Yankees were "full as bad as the Indians for scalping and cutting the dead men's ears and noses off."[15]) Adams could hardly wait for Congress to regroup and quickly left his sick bed.

On my return home, I was seized with a fever, attended with alarming symptoms; but the time was come to repair to Philadelphia to Congress, which was to meet on the [10th] of May. I was determined to go as far as I could, and instead of venturing on horseback, as I had intended, I got into a sulky, attended by a servant [Joseph Bass] ... and proceeded on the journey. This year, [John] Hancock was added to our number. I overtook my colleagues before they reached New York. At Kingsbridge we were met by a great number of gentlemen in carriages and on horseback, and all the way their numbers increased, till I thought the whole city was come out to meet us.[16]

> The tumult frightened the mare, wrecked the sulky, and risked his ailing life, but Adams soldiered on.[17] He now saw armed rebellion as the sole cure for a diseased system.

The general sense abroad is, to prepare for a vigorous defensive war, but at the same time to keep open the door of reconciliation; to hold the sword in one hand and the olive branch in the other. . . . I am myself as fond of

Maneuvering Independence

reconciliation, if we could reasonably entertain hopes of it upon a constitutional basis, as any man. But I think . . . the cancer is too deeply rooted and too far spread to be cured by any thing short of cutting it out entire.[18]

> He grew more anxious and angry with reports from besieged Boston, particularly when he heard of Dr. Joseph Warren's being fatally bayoneted as he lay wounded on Bunker Hill. Adams chafed at Congress's deliberate inaction.

It appeared to me that all petitions, remonstrances, and negotiations, for the future, would be fruitless, and only occasion a loss of time, and give opportunity to the enemy to sow divisions among the States and the people. My heart bled for the poor people of Boston, imprisoned within the walls of their city by a British army, and we knew not to what plunders or massacres or cruelties they might be exposed.[19]

> He proposed a plan to 1) take officers of the Crown hostage for Bostonians' safety; 2) have each state institute its own government; 3) declare the Colonies "free, sovereign, and independent States"; 4) offer to negotiate for redress of grievances, while warning of possible alliances with European powers; and 5) establish a united continental army.[20] The plan provoked instant opposition from conservative members.

From conversation with the members of Congress, I was then convinced, . . . that it was the general sense of a considerable majority of that body. This system of measures I publicly and privately avowed without reserve. . . . In some of my public harangues, in which I had freely and explicitly laid open my thoughts, on looking round the assembly I have seen horror, terror, and detestation, strongly marked on some of the members. . . .[21] There was a little aristocracy among us, of talents and letters; Mr. [John] Dickinson was *primus inter pares*, the bellwether, the leader of the aristocratical flock.[22]

> Adams concurred with the principles of forty-two-year-old, tall, cadaverous John Dickinson, author of the influential "Farmer's Letters," but despised his policy of appeasement. He ridiculed the celebrated "Penman of the Revolution" as one whose time had passed.[23]

Mr. Charles Thomson, who was then rather inclined to our side of the question, told me that the Quakers had intimidated Mr. Dickinson's mother and his wife, who were continually distressing him with their remonstrances. His mother said to him, "Johnny, you will be hanged; your estate will be forfeited and confiscated; you will leave your excellent wife a widow, and your charming children orphans, beggars, and infamous." From my soul I pitied Mr. Dickinson. I made his case my own. If my mother and my wife had expressed such sentiments to me, I was certain that if they did not wholly unman me and make me an apostate, they would make me the most miserable man alive.[24]

> Adams was too quick to accept this hearsay. The Dickinsons were not pacifist Quakers. Younger brother Philemon became a general and John, at forty-four, a colonel[25]—a better statesman than soldier, sniffed querulous Adams.

I have felt such passions all my lifetime, particularly in the year 1757, when I longed to be a more ardently soldier than I ever did to be a lawyer. But I am too old [at forty], and too much worn with fatigues of study in my youth, and there is too little need . . . for me to assume a uniform.[26]

Maneuvering Independence

In Philadelphia's State House yard, in fact, the Adams cousins were boldly conspiring to nominate Virginian George Washington as head of a unified military command.

"What shall we do to get Congress to adopt our army?" said Samuel Adams to John Adams.

"I will tell you what I am determined to do," said John to Samuel. "I have taken pains enough to bring you to agree upon something, but you will not agree upon any thing, and now I am determined to take my own way, let come what will."

"Well," said Samuel, "what is your scheme?"

Said John to Samuel, "I will go to Congress this morning, and move, that a day be appointed to take into consideration the adoption of the army before Boston, the appointment of a General, and officers; and I will nominate Washington for commander-in-chief."[27]

When Congress had assembled, I rose in my place, and in as short a speech as the subject would admit, represented the state of the Colonies, the uncertainty in the minds of the people, their great expectation and anxiety, the distresses of the [militia at Boston], the danger of its dissolution, the difficulty of collecting another, and the probability that the British army would take advantage of our delays, march out of Boston, and spread desolation as far as they could go. I concluded with a motion, in form, that Congress would adopt the army at Cambridge, and appoint a General. . . . I had no hesitation to declare that I had but one gentleman in my mind for that important command, and that was a gentleman from Virginia, who was among us and very well known to all of us, a gentleman whose skill and experience as an officer, whose independent fortune, great talents, and excellent universal character, would command the approbation of all America, and unite the cordial exertions of all the Colonies better than any other person in the Union. Mr. Washington, who happened to sit near the door, as soon as he heard me allude to him, from his usual modesty, darted into the library-room.... Pains were taken out of doors to obtain a unanimity.[28]

> Though pleased with his performance, Adams nevertheless felt unfulfilled as he escorted Washington's triumphal procession out of town en route to Cambridge. The success would have been sweeter had it not been delayed too long.

All the delegates from the Massachusetts, with their servants and carriages, attended; many others of the delegates from the Congress; a large troop of light horse in their uniforms; many officers of militia besides, in theirs; music playing, etc. etc. Such is the pride and pomp of war. I, poor creature, worn out with scribbling for my bread and my liberty, low in spirits and weak in health, must leave others to wear the laurels which I have sown; others to eat the bread which I have earned.[29]

They had not proceeded twenty miles from Philadelphia, before they met a courier with the news of the battle of Bunker's Hill, the death of General Warren, the slaughter among the British officers and men, as well as among ours, and the burning of Charlestown.

I have always imputed the loss of Charlestown, and of the brave officers and men who fell there, and the loss of a hero of more worth than all the town, I mean General Warren, to Mr. Dickinson's petition to the King ... and to his subsequent, unceasing, though finally unavailing efforts against independence. These impeded and paralyzed all our enterprises ... every measure was delayed, till it became ineffectual.

Maneuvering Independence

In the fall of the year, Congress was much fatigued with the incessant labors, debates, intrigues, and heats of the summer, and agreed on a short adjournment.[30]

6

DECLARING INDEPENDENCE

1775–1776

The means to oppose John Dickinson's "unceasing efforts ... against independence"[1] came from a quarter-century's study of legal history. The motive came from a clash of personalities. Dickinson's open disdain and public intimidation angered Adams into a careless mistake requiring redoubled zeal for Independence.

> [*16 September 1775*] Walking to the State House this morning, I met Mr. Dickinson, on foot, in Chesnut Street. We met, and passed near enough to touch elbows. He passed without moving his hat or head or hand. I bowed, and pulled off my hat. He passed haughtily by. . . . I shall, for the future, pass him in the same manner; but I was determined to make my bow, that I might know his temper.[2]

> A soul sensitive to criticism of any kind bruised more readily under stress. Word came that Braintree was under a two-month siege of dysentery; the cozy homestead was now a busy hospital. Also infected, yet continuing to nurse others, Abigail Adams struggled with the loss of her mother to the disease. She was devastated—with John Adams three hundred miles away.[3] Heading homeward, he learned of a more intimate victim of that same scourge.

Adjournment of Congress, for a few weeks, in the fall of 1775 gave me ... the hopes of seeing my family for a few days. Arriving, on horseback, from Philadelphia, within a quarter of a mile of my house, I met an acquaintance, who informed me that my favourite brother [twenty-five-year-old Elihu], who had commanded a company of volunteers in the army at Cambridge from the 19th of April, and there taken the camp dissentary, lay at the point of death, given over by his physicians. Buoyed up with the joyous hope of embracing my wife and children in a few minutes, how was I cast down? The next morning brought the fatal news of his death. I attended his funeral; and all the joy of my visit home, was turned into mourning![4]

> On 28 October 1775, the provincial government named John Adams chief justice of Massachusetts, vindicating his crusade against Hutchinson's courts, validating his program for Independence, capping his twenty years of life in law, and giving him another good excuse—besides care and comfort of family—to stay home.

By retreating from public life, in some measure I might preserve myself and family from a ruin, which without it would be inevitable. I am willing to sink with my country, but it ought not to be insisted on that I should sink myself without prospect of contributing by that means to make it swim. I have taken my trick at helm when it was not easy to get navigators who would run the risque of the storm. At present the course is plain whatever the weather may be, and the prospect of that is much better than it was when I was called to assist upon steering the ship.[5]

> He could not ignore national responsibility. Other states sought his aid in modeling constitutions after the one with balanced powers that he had drawn for Massachusetts. He

Declaring Independence

composed a guide, eventually printed as a twenty-eight-page pamphlet, *Thoughts on Government*.

All those who were the most zealous for assuming governments, had at that time no idea of any other government but a contemptible legislature in one assembly, with committees for executive magistrates and judges.... I had read Harrington, Sidney, Hobbes, Nedham, and Locke, but with little application to any particular views, till these debates in Congress, and the interrogatories in public and private ("What plan of government would you recommend?"), turned my thoughts to these researches, which produced the "Thoughts on Government," the Constitution of Massachusetts, and at length the "Defence of the Constitutions of the United States," and the "Discourses on Davila," writings which have never done any good to me, though some of them undoubtedly contributed to produce the Constitution of New York, the Constitution of the United States, and the last Constitutions of Pennsylvania and Georgia. They undoubtedly also contributed to the writings of Publius, called the Federalist, which were all written after the publication of my work in Philadelphia, New York, and Boston.[6]

> Despite long-range influence, the *Thoughts on Government* met immediate competition from Thomas Paine's fifty-eight-page *Common Sense*. Paine at thirty-seven, hawk nosed, wiry, recently arrived from England, called for a complete break but a unicameral legislature and weak executive. Adams fumed.

Such a mongrel between piggs and puppy, begotten by a wild boar on a bitch wolf, never before in any Age of the World was suffered by the poltroonery of mankind, to run through such a career of mischief.[7]

Paine raged against "The Royal Brute of England" with "blood upon his soul"[8] in language Adams heard from street mobs. He was more shocked that Paine viewed him as Adams viewed Dickinson and *Thoughts on Government* as a speed trap on the road to revolution. Adams read *Common Sense* as sharing "Arguments which [Adams] had been repeating again and again in Congress for nine months."[9]

Paine, soon after the appearance of my pamphlet, hurried away to my lodgings and spent an evening with me. His business was to reprehend me for publishing my pamphlet; said he was afraid it would do hurt, and that it was repugnant to the plan he had proposed in his *Common Sense.* I told him it was true it was repugnant, and for that reason I had written it and consented to the publication of it; for I was as much afraid of his work as he was of mine. His plan was so democratical, without any restraints or even an attempt at any equilibrium or counterpoise, that it must produce confusion and every evil work.... This conversation passed in good humor, without any harshness on either side.[10]

> Adams feared that Paine's intemperate style "had as much weight with the people as his arguments" and blamed the backlash for fortifying and inflaming "the party against independence."[11]

It is the fate of men and things which do great good that they always do great evil too. "Common sense," by his crude ignorant notion of a government by one assembly, will do more mischief, in dividing the friends of liberty, than all the Tory writings together. He is a keen writer but very ignorant of the science of government.[12]

> But to Abigail Adams he confided a sense of genial envy.

This writer has a better hand in pulling down than

Declaring Independence

building. It has been very generally propagated through the continent that I wrote this pamphlet. But although I could not have written anything in so manly and striking a style, I flatter myself I should have made a more respectable figure as an architect, if I had undertaken such a work.[13]

> The patriotism fanned by *Common Sense* also fueled Adams's sense of being needed by the nation. He relinquished his seat as Chief Justice without ever having sat upon the bench and hazarded health, happiness, family, and fortune to go back to Congress.

I have ever considered the confidence of the public the more honorable in proportion to the perplexity and danger of the times.[14] I was determined, whilst I was ruining my constitution, both of mind and body, and running daily risks of my life and fortune in defence of the independence of my country, I would not knowingly resign my own.[15]

> Abigail Adams, sensing a genial mood, teased him with her celebrated ultimatum: "Remember the ladies. . . . If particular care and attention is not paid to the ladies, we are determined to foment a rebellion, and will not hold ourselves bound by any laws in which we have no voice or representation."[16] Adams responded in kind.

We have only the name of masters, and rather than give up this, which would completely subject us to the despotism of the petticoat, I hope General Washington and all our brave heroes would fight. . . . I begin to think the ministry as deep as they are wicked. After stirring up Tories, land-jobbers, trimmers, bigots, Canadians, Indians, negroes, Hanoverians, Hessians, Russians, Irish Roman Catholics, Scotch renegadoes, at last they have stimulated the —— to demand new privileges and threaten to rebel.[17]

With the British evacuating Boston, Adams could relax vigilance against British arms and enjoy himself. But his zeal fanned Dickinson's fury for delay.

Mr. Dickinson made or procured to be made a motion for a second petition to the King . . . introduced and supported by long speeches. I was opposed to it, of course, and made an opposition to it in as long a speech as I commonly made, not having ever been remarkable for very long harangues, in answer to all the arguments which had been urged. . . . Mr. Dickinson, very much terrified at [support for Adams] began to tremble for his cause. At this moment I was called out to the State House yard, very much to my regret, to some one who had business with me. I took my hat, and went out of the door of Congress Hall.

> Dickinson, lanky and cadaverous as Don Quixote, caught paunchy, stocky Adams in the public courtyard.

Mr. Dickinson observed me, and darted out after me. He broke out upon me in a most abrupt and extraordinary manner; in as violent a passion as he was capable of feeling, and with an air, countenance, and gestures, as rough and haughty as if I had been a school-boy and he the master. . . .

"What is the reason, Mr. Adams, that you New-Englandmen oppose our measures of reconciliation? There now is [John] Sullivan, in a long harangue, following you in a determined opposition to our petition to the King. Look ye! If you don't concur with us in our pacific system, I and a number of us will break off from you in New England, and we will carry on the opposition by ourselves in our own way."

I own I was shocked with this magisterial salutation. I knew of no pretensions Mr. Dickinson had to dictate to me, more than I had to catechize him. I was, however, as it

Declaring Independence

happened, at that moment, in a very happy temper, and I answered him very cooly. "Mr. Dickinson, there are many things that I can very cheerfully sacrifice to harmony, and even to unanimity; but I am not to be threatened into an express adoption or approbation of measures which my judgment reprobates. Congress must judge, and if they pronounce against me, I must submit, as, if they determine against you, you ought to acquiesce."

> Predisposed to seething anger, Adams boiled over in letters (as he had earlier warned Abigail Adams, open to interception) that leaked the plans for Independence.

The more I reflected on Mr. Dickinson's rude lecture in the State House yard, the more I was vexed with it; and the determination of Congress in favor of the petition did not allay the irritation. A young gentleman from Boston, [Benjamin] Hichborn . . . with whom I had no particular connnection or acquaintance, had been for some days soliciting me to give him letters to my friends in the Massachusetts. . . . To get rid of his importunity, I took my pen and wrote a very few lines . . . to General James Warren.

Philadelphia, 24 July 1775.

Dear Sir:—I am determined to write freely to you this time. A certain great fortune and piddling genius, whose fame has been trumpeted so loudly, has given a silly cast to our whole doings. We are between hawk and buzzard. We ought to have had in our hands, a month ago, the whole legislative, executive, and judicial of the whole continent, and have completely modelled a constitution; to have raised a naval power, and opened all our ports wide; to have arrested every friend of government on the continent and held them as hostages for the poor victims in Boston, and then opened the door as wide as possible for peace and reconciliation....

Mr. Hichborn was intercepted in crossing Hudson's River, by the boats from a British man-of-war, and my letters, instead of being destroyed, fell into the hands of the enemy, and were immediately printed with a little garbling. They thought them a great prize.

> He had accused *Common Sense* of harming the cause, but the intercepted letters had also cost public support and had created a serious split in Congress. Yet, Adams managed to rationalize his error in judgment as a public service.

From this time, at least, if not earlier, and not from the publication of "Common Sense," did the people in all parts of the continent turn their attention to this subject.... It was happy that the whole country had been compelled to turn their thoughts upon [independence], that it might not come upon them by surprise.[18]

> Apparently his zeal in committee work deflected congressional censure. In mid-May, Adams prepared the unanimous resolution "for assuming government in all the colonies."[19] A month later, he joined the committee to draft a declaration of independence chaired by Thomas Jefferson. Jefferson's erudition and zeal along with self-deprecating modesty attracted Adams at first sight.

Mr. Jefferson came into Congress in June 1775 and brought with him a reputation for literature, science, and a happy talent at composition. Writings of his were handed about, remarkable for the peculiar felicity of expression.[20] During the whole time I sat with him in Congress, I never heard him utter three sentences together.... Though a silent member in Congress, he was so prompt, frank, explicit, and decisive upon committees and in conversation, not even Samuel Adams was more so, that he soon seized upon my heart.[21] Jefferson, in those days, never failed to agree with me, in every thing of a political nature.[22] Jefferson was but a boy to me. I was at least ten years older than him in age and more than twenty years older than him in politics. I am bold to say I was his preceptor in politics and taught him everything that has been good and solid in his whole political conduct.[23]

> Jefferson already had a good solid reputation with his influential *Summary View of the Rights of British America* (1774). Pale, stout Adams and ruddy, six-foot-two, lanky Jefferson bonded in mutual admiration. Jefferson, in old age, told an interviewer, "John Adams was our Colossus on the floor. He was not graceful, nor elegant, nor remarkably fluent; but he came out occasionally with a power of thought and expression, that moved us from our seats."[24] Adams, in like old age, confessed to friends, "I always loved Jefferson and still love him."[25]

Jefferson proposed to me to make the draught. I said, "I will not."
"You should do it."
"Oh! no."
"Why will you not? You ought to do it."
"I will not."
"Why?"
"Reasons enough."
"What can be your reasons?"
"Reason first—You are a Virginian, and a Virginian ought to appear at the head of this business. Reason second—I am obnoxious, suspected, and unpopular. You are

very much otherwise. Reason third—You can write ten times better than I can...."

I was delighted with its high tone and the flights of oratory with which it abounded, especially that concerning negro slavery, which, though I knew his Southern brethren would never suffer to pass in Congress, I certainly never would oppose. There were other expressions which I would not have inserted, if I had drawn it up, particularly that which called the King a tyrant. I thought *this* too personal. ... the expression too passionate, and too much like scolding, for so grave and solemn a document; but as Franklin and Sherman were to inspect it afterwards, I thought it would not become me to strike it out. I consented to report it, and do not now remember that I made or suggested a single alteration.[26]

> With Dickinson absent leading militia to camp, the Declaration passed unanimously on 2 July. Published copies appeared two days later. The familiar engrossed copy would be signed by delegates, except Dickinson, in August.

The second day of July, 1776, will be the most memorable epocha in the history of America. I am apt to believe that it will be celebrated by succeeding generations as the great anniversary festival. It ought to be commemorated as the day of deliverance, by solemn acts of devotion to God Almighty. It ought to be solemnized with pomp and parade, with shows, games, sports, guns, bells, bonfires, and illuminations, from one end of this continent to the other, from this time forward evermore.

You will think me transported with enthusiasm, but I am not. I am well aware of the toil and blood and treasure that it will cost us to maintain this declaration and support and defend these States. Yet, through all the gloom, I can

Declaring Independence

see the rays of ravishing light and glory. I can see that the end is more than worth all the means. And that posterity will triumph in that day's transaction, even although we should rue it, which I trust in God we shall not.[27]

> Jefferson's methodical mind tempered Adams's impetuosity on other committee work—as in revising the Articles of War that governed discipline in the armed forces, for which they ultimately adopted the British model.[28] But devising the Articles of Confederation took sixteen months, with Colonel Dickinson leading a successful charge for a strong legislature, weak executive, and voting by states rather than population. Adams conceded defeat.

He sat and appeared full of thought. He rose. "Mr. President." His cane slipped through his thumb and forefinger, with a quick tap upon the floor; his eyes rolled upwards; his brows were raised to their full arch. "This business, sir, that has taken up so much of our time seems to be finished. But, sir, I now, upon this floor, venture to predict that, before ten years, this confederation, like a rope of sand, will be found inadequate to the purpose, and its dissolution will take place.[29]

> Adams was sent to a conference with Lord Richard Howe at Staten Island. Edward Rutledge and Franklin rode in carriages while Adams rode horseback. Having to share a bed, Franklin tricked Adams into sleeping with an open window.

Monday, September 9 [1776]. At Brunswick, but one bed could be procured for Dr. Franklin and me, in a chamber little larger than the bed, without a chimney, and with only one small window. The window was open, and I, who was an invalid and afraid of the air in the night, shut it close. "Oh!" says Franklin, "don't shut the window, we shall be suffocated."

I answered, I was afraid of the evening air.

Dr. Franklin replied, "The air within this chamber will soon be, and indeed is now, worse than that without doors. Come, open the window and come to bed, and I will convince you. I believe you are not acquainted with my theory of colds."

Opening the window and leaping into bed, I said I had read his letters to Dr. [Samuel] Cooper, in which he had advanced, that nobody ever got cold by going into a cold church or any other cold air, but the theory was so little consistent with my experience, that I thought it a paradox. However, I had so much curiosity to hear his reasons that I would run the risk of a cold.

The Doctor then began a harangue upon air and cold, and respiration and perspiration, with which I was so much amused that I soon fell asleep, and left him and his philosophy together.[30]

> As the conference concluded with more said than done, Adams's patience yielded to his caustic wit.

When his lordship observed to us, that he could not confer with us as members of Congress, or public characters, but only as private persons and British subjects, Mr. John Adams answered somewhat quickly, "Your lordship may consider me in what light you please, and, indeed, I should be willing to consider myself, for a few moments, in any character which would be agreeable to your lordship, *except that of a British subject.*"[31]

I left Congress on the 11th of November, 1777 . . . just as Congress had gone through the confederation but before it was signed. . . . I own I gave up that confederation in despair of its efficacy or long utility.[32]

7

PRACTICING DIPLOMACY

1776–1780

Despite the way his intercepted letters exposed their proceedings, Congress found Adams invaluable as a moderating influence on the many regional and political factions in committees. He served on ninety committees, chairing forty with diplomacy that would be put into service overseas. Meanwhile he was named to head the most important committee, the five-member Board of War and Ordnance. He enjoyed the challenge of civilians conducting the war.

It is a great mortification to me, I confess, and I fear it will too often be a misfortune to our country, that I am called to the discharge of trusts to which I feel myself so unequal, and in the execution of which I can derive no assistance from my education or former course of life. But my country must command me, and wherever she shall order me, there I will go without dismay.[1]

In fact, a month of chairing the Board during a Philadelphia summer almost ruined his health.

The increasing heat of the weather, added to incessant application to business without any intermissions of exercise, has relaxed me to such a degree that a few weeks more would totally incapacitate me for any thing.... My face has grown pale, my eyes weak and inflamed, my nerves tremulous, and my mind weak as water—feverish heats by day and sweats by night are returned upon me, which is an infallible symptom with me that it is time to throw off all care for a time and take a little rest. I have several times with the blessing of God saved my life in this way.[2]

> But there was a war on. His Board administered manpower, money, and materiel. They raised, supported, and transported troops; kept accounts of arms, ammunition, and supplies in each colony; acted as liaison for colonies, army, and Congress—all by persuasion alone. Adams had little time or energy to write home.

From four o'clock in the morning until ten at night, I have not a single moment which I can call my own. I will not say that I expect to run distracted, to grow melancholy, to drop in an apoplexy, or fall into a consumption; but I do say, it is little less than a miracle that one or the other of these misfortunes has not befallen me before now.[3]

The duties of this Board kept me in continual employment not to say drudgery from the Twelfth of June 1776 till the Eleventh of November 1777, when I left Congress forever. Not only my mornings and evenings were filled with the crowd of business before the Board, but a great part of my time in Congress was engaged in making, explaining, and justifying our reports and proceedings.... Other gentlemen attended as they pleased, but as I was Chairman, or as they were pleased to call it, President, I must never be absent.[4]

> In February 1777, Abigail Adams wrote to him from bed. Even as she was miscarrying a baby girl she wrote on, "—and

Practicing Diplomacy

now I have endured it I reassume my pen."[5] With draft of local men into the army, she worked in the fields. She confessed, "I should make a poor figure at digging potatoes."[6] Her plaintive voice finally overwhelmed his stern sense of duty, but not for long.

When I asked leave of Congress to make a visit to my constituents and my family in November 1777, it was my intention to decline the next election, and return to my practice at the bar. I had been four years in Congress, had left my accounts in a very loose condition, my debtors were failing, the paper money was depreciating; I was daily losing the fruits of seventeen years' industry; my family was living on my past acquisitions, which were very moderate, for no man ever did so much business for so little profit; my children were growing up without my care in their education, and all my emoluments as a member of Congress, for four years, had not been sufficient to pay a laboring man upon my farm.

> Adams picked up family life more easily than he could hold onto it. On the circuit, he learned Congress wanted to send him to France for aid. Though he had no experience abroad, no one knew better how badly the Revolution needed money and military assistance. He grappled with guilt over abandoning his family. That the appointment was unsolicited and was by popular demand made his choice inevitable.

My family, consisting of a dearly beloved wife and four young children, excited sentiments of tenderness, which a father and a lover only can conceive, and which no language can express; and my want of qualifications for the office was by no means forgotten.

On the other hand, my country was in deep distress

and in great danger. Her dearest interests would be involved in the relations she might form with foreign nations. My own plan of these relations [in a model treaty] had been deliberately formed and fully communicated to Congress nearly two years before. The confidence of my country was committed to me without my solicitation. My wife, who had always encouraged and animated me in all antecedent dangers and perplexities, did not fail me on this occasion. But she discovered an inclination to bear me company, with all our children. This proposal, however, she was soon convinced, was too hazardous and imprudent.... After much agitation of mind, and a thousand reveries unnecessary to be detailed, I resolved to devote my family and my life to the cause, accepted the appointment, and made preparations for the voyage.[7]

> He did not worry about the North Atlantic during winter on the frigate *Boston* or about being captured for treason. He was more concerned about taking their nine-year-old son, John Quincy, to continue abroad the schooling that had been interrupted by war at home. Adams even had him tutored at sea.

February 17. Tuesday 1778. I set a lesson to my son in Chambaud's French Grammar, and asked the favor of Dr. [Nicholas] Noel [ship's surgeon] to show him the precise, critical pronunciation of all the French words, syllables, and letters, which the Doctor very politely did, and Mr. John is getting his lessons accordingly, very much pleased.

February 25. Wednesday 1778. [After four days of evading enemy ships and of being battered by hurricane-force storms] I was myself perfectly calm, during the whole. I found, by the opinion of the people aboard, and of the captain himself, that we were in danger, and of this I was certain also, from my own observation; but I thought myself in the way of my duty, and I did not repent of my voyage. I confess I often regretted that I had brought my son. I was not so clear that it was my duty to expose him as myself, but I had been led to it by the child's inclination, and by the advice of all my friends. Mr Johnny's behavior gave me a satisfaction that I cannot express; fully sensible of our danger, he was constantly endeavoring to bear it with manly patience, very attentive to me, and his thoughts constantly running in a serious strain.

March 3, Tuesday 1778. The life I lead is a dull scene to me; no business, no pleasure, no study. Our little world is all wet and damp. There is nothing I can eat or drink without nauseating. We have no spirits for conversation, nor any thing to converse about. We see nothing but sky, clouds, and sea, and then sea, clouds, and sky.[8]

> He was bored until the *Boston* encountered the enemy ship *Martha*. On deck, musket in hand, he fought fiercely as a common marine. Ordered below, he went on firing until Captain Samuel Tucker "forcibly carried" him to safety.[9] He enjoyed the heroic fame until 1 April, when they reached Bordeaux. There the natives welcomed him as "Sam Adams," celebrated author of *Common Sense*.

> When I arrived at Bordeaux, all that I could say or do would not convince anybody but that I was the *fameux* Adams. "C'est un homme célèbre. Votre nom est bien connu ici." ["A celebrity! Your name is well known here."]
> My answer was, "It is another gentleman, whose name of Adams you have heard; it is Mr. Samuel Adams...."

"Oh non, Monsieur, c'est votre modestie."

But when I arrived at Paris, I found a very different style. I found great pains taken, much more than the question was worth, to settle the point that I was not the famous Adams. There was a dread of a sensation; sensations at Paris are important things. I soon found, too, that it was effectually settled in the English newspapers that I was not the famous Adams. Nobody went so far in France or England as to say that I was the *infamous* Adams....

The consequence was settled, absolutely and unalterably, that I was a man of whom nobody had ever heard before—a perfect cipher; a man who did not understand a word of French; awkward in his figure, awkward in his dress; no abilities; a perfect bigot and fanatic.[10]

> He converted the confusion into charming table talk (via an interpreter) with a woman curious about family matters.

"Mr. Adams, by your name I conclude you are descended from the first man and woman, and probably in your family may be preserved the tradition which may resolve a difficulty which I could never explain. I never could understand how the first couple found out the art of lying together?..."

Composing my countenance into an ironical gravity I answered her,... "The subject was perfectly understood by us, whether by tradition I could not tell: I rather thought it was by instinct, for there was a physical quality in us resembling the power of electricity or of the magnet, by which when a pair approached within striking distance they flew together like the [compass] needle to the pole or like two objects in electric experiments."

When this answer was explained to her [by the interpreter], she replied, "Well, I know not how it was, but this I know—it is a very happy shock."[11]

Practicing Diplomacy

He could jest about his name but not about personal slights. He found that his presence was superfluous. A treaty with France had been signed while he was still at sea, and he had nothing to do. His colleagues, Arthur Lee and Benjamin Franklin, feuded fiercely. Upset by their neglect, Adams tried in vain to mediate.[12]

I found that the business of our Commission would never be done unless I did it. My two colleagues would agree in nothing. The life of Dr. Franklin was a scene of continual discipation. I could never obtain the favour of his company in a morning before breakfast which would have been the most convenient time to read over the letters and papers, deliberate on their contents, and decide upon the substance of the answers. It was late when he breakfasted, and as soon as breakfast was over, a crowd of carriges came to his levee or if you like the term better to his lodgings, with all sorts of people. . . . I should have been happy to have done all the business or rather all the drudgery, if I could have been favoured with a few moments in a day to receive his advice concerning the manner in which it ought to be done. But this condescention was not attainable.[13]

> To feel useful, Adams used his accounting skills to straighten out the legation's bookkeeping.

The public business has never been methodically conducted. There never was, before I came, a minute book, a letter book, or an account book. . . . or, if there had been, Mr. Deane and Dr. Franklin had concealed them from Mr. Lee, and they were now nowhere to be found. It was utterly impossible to acquire any clear idea of our affairs. I was now determined to procure some blank books and to apply myself with diligence to business, in which Mr. Lee cordially joined me.[14]

Franklin introduced Adams to Foreign Minister Vergennes and twenty-four-year-old King Louis XVI, who awed Adams.

> His Majesty turned about, towards me, and smiled. "Est-ce Monsieur Adams?" said the King, and then asked a question very quick, or rather made an observation to me, which I did not fully understand. The purport of it was, that I had not been long arrived. The Count Vergennes then conducted me to the door of another room, and desired me to stand there, which I did, until the King passed. The Count told the King that I did not yet take upon me to speak French. The King asked, whether I did not speak *at all*.[15]

Adams feelings toward Franklin were ambivalent at best. He would play his Boswell in recording Franklin's stories[16] but make acid comments on his popularity with the French—as at the prestigious Academy of Sciences when octogenarian Voltaire and septuagenarian Franklin were introduced.

29 April 1778. This was done, and they bowed and spoke to each other. This was no satisfaction; there must be something more. Neither of our philosophers seemed to divine what was wished or expected; they, however, took each other by the hand. But this was not enough; the clamor continued, until the explanation came out. "Il faut s'embrasser, à la Françoise." [They must embrace, French style.]

The two aged actors upon this great theatre of philosophy and frivolity then embraced each other, by hugging one another in their arms and kissing each other's cheeks, and then the tumult subsided. And the cry immediately spread through the whole kingdom, and, I suppose, over all Europe. "Qu'il etait charmant de voir embrasser Solon et Sophocle!" [How charming to have seen Solon and Sophocles embrace!][17]

Practicing Diplomacy

Chafing from inaction, Adams began writing to Vergennes criticizing his policies and to Congress about Franklin's mismanagement. Vergennes, suspecting Adams of being pro-British,[18] complained to Congress, but Adams persevered.

> [Arthur Lee] has given offence by an unhappy disposition, and by indiscreet speeches before servants and others, concerning the French nation and government—despising and cursing them. I am sorry for these things, but it is no part of my business to quarrel with anybody without cause; it is no part of my duty to differ with one party or another, or to give offence to anybody; but I must do my duty to the public, let it give offence to whom it will.[19]

Fed up, Adams urged Congress to reform the entire commission. They did so by appointing Franklin the sole commissioner, leaving Adams in limbo for more than nine months, vulnerable to infection from Lee's paranoia.

> They never so much as bid me come home, bid me stay, or told me I had done well or done ill... You know not, you feel not, the dangers that surround me nor those that may be brought upon our country.... There are spies upon every word I utter, and every syllable I write. Spies planted by the English, spies planted by stock-jobbers, spies planted by selfish merchants, and spies planted by envious and malicious politicians. I have been all along aware of this, more or less, but more so now than ever. My life has been often in danger, but I never considered my reputation and character so much in danger as now.[20]

Delayed from going home from March until June 1779, Adams felt "more miserable than ever I was."[21] He was set to sail on the American frigate *Alliance*. At the last minute Franklin ordered him to wait for the French frigate *Sensible*—thus reinforcing his suspicion of conspiracy.

Does the old conjuror dread my voice in Congress?[22]

At the King's invitation, Adams sailed with new ambassador Chevalier de la Luzerne to America,.[23] Other than furthering John Quincy's education, Adams's first year abroad gained little.

> My son has had a great opportunity to see this country; but this has unavoidably retarded his education in some other things. He has enjoyed perfect health, from first to last, and is respected wherever he goes, for his vigor and vivacity both of mind and body, for his constant good humor, and for his rapid progress in French as well as his general knowledge, which, for his age, is uncommon.[24]

On the forty-seven-day voyage home, Adams proudly watched John Quincy teach English to Luzerne's entourage, just as the boy had learned French aboard the *Boston*. Approaching American waters infested with British naval forces, John Adams found himself wrapped in a symbolic friendly fog.

At the moment I am writing, a thick fog comes up on all sides, as if directed specially to conceal us from our enemies. I am not so presumptuous as to flatter myself that these happy circumstances are all ordered for the preservation of this frigate, but not to remark them would be stupidity, not to rejoice in them would be ingratitude. If we should be prospered so much as to arrive well, what news shall we find public or private?[25]

After hardly a month's cuddling with his family and calculating damage to his farm, Adams went to the Massachusetts constitutional convention (1 September 1779). Smarting from the past year's intrigue, he would no longer suffer expedients gladly.

Practicing Diplomacy

I found such a chaos of absurd sentiments concerning government that I was obliged daily before that great assembly, and afterwards in the grand committee, to propose plans and advocate doctrines which were extremely unpopular with the greater number.

> Adams won provisions for freedom of religion. He now proposed restoring a strong executive with the power to veto appointments—just such as Hutchinson had employed against Adams himself.

I had at first no support but from [those] who had adopted my ideas in [*Thoughts on Government*]. They supported me timorously and at last would not go with me to so high a mark as I aimed at, which was a complete negative [veto] in the governor upon all laws. They made me, however, draw up the constitution, and it was finally adopted with some amendments very much for the worse.

The bold, decided, and determined part I took in this assembly in favor of a good government, acquired me the reputation of a man of high principles and strong notions in government, scarcely compatible with republicanism. A foundation was here laid of much jealousy and unpopularity among the democratical people in this state.[26]

> He was spared listening to the convention mangle his plan. Congress sent him back to Paris seeking a commercial treaty with Britain, again on the *Sensible*, this time with John Quincy and nine-year-old Charles. Upon reaching Spain, the old *Sensible* sprung a leak. Impatient, the Adams party traveled to Paris by a decrepit, mule-drawn buggy—beneath the dignity of an American ambassador.

30 January 1780. A fertile country, not half cultivated, people ragged and dirty, and the houses universally nothing but mire, smoke, fleas, and lice. Nothing appears rich but the churches; nobody fat but the clergy.[27]

> Their welcome in France was polite, friendly, and properly respectful except that Vergennes advised against letting the British know his mission while war raged. Adams complied unwillingly.

If I had followed my own judgment, I should have pursued a bolder plan; by communicating, immediately after my arrival, to Lord George Germaine [colonial secretary], my full powers to treat both of peace and commerce: but ... I think no doubt can be made, that it is my duty to conduct my negotiations at present in concert with our ally.[28]

> In Paris, the British, not recognizing America's independence, did not recognize Adams's office. Chafing at inactivity, he would write letters criticizing French policy. Vergennes, finally fed up with Adams's "too ardent imagination,"[29] his stubborness, and his threats, cut him off: "Mr. Franklin being the sole person who has letters of credence to the king from the United States, it is with him only that I ought and can treat."[30]

I had so uniformly resisted all the arts and intrigues of the Count de Vergennes ... and all their satellites, and that with such perfect success that I well knew, although they treated me with great external respect, yet in their hearts they had conceived an ineradicable jealousy and aversion to me. I well knew, therefore, that French influence in America would do all in its power to trip me up.[31]

> At the end of 1780, Vergennes asked Congress to remove Adams. Congress responded six months later by enlarging the peace commission. By then he was happy to leave Paris—for the boys' sake.

Practicing Diplomacy

There is everything [in Paris] that can inform the understanding or refine the taste, and indeed, one would think, that could purify the heart. Yet it must be remembered there is everything too which can seduce, betray, deceive, deprave, corrupt, and debauch it. Hercules marches here in full view of the steeps of virtue on one hand and the flowery paths of pleasure on the other, and there are few who make the choice of Hercules. That my children may follow his example is my earnest prayer; but I sometimes tremble when I hear the siren song of sloth, lest they should be captivated with her bewitching charms and her soft, insinuating music.[32]

Adams sallied forth seeking loans at the Hague.

8

BECOMING THE "WASHINGTON OF NEGOTIATION"

1781–1783

Adams knew no Dutch, yet he hoped to secure loans at the Hague. But if the Dutch government negotiated with him, they faced British reprisals. He would persevere for a year against Congress, Franklin, and the French in order to win recognition from the Dutch directly along with a commercial treaty and loans to keep the Revolution alive. Peace would restore his health and his hope of a reunion with his family—both were interrupted by the need to secure more loans.

I wish I were at home that I might do something worthy of History. Here I can do nothing. The beauteous olive branch, I fear, will never decorate my brows. I must spend my life in the pride, pomp and circumstance of glorious war, without sharing any of its laurels. . . . There are in my power means enough for the pursuit of pleasure and of knowledge; but I have not that inclination to take the advantage of them, which I should have done in earlier life, before my soul was bowed down with care.[1]

The black cloud that hung over the whole of the seven

[Dutch] provinces; the solemn gloom that pervaded the whole nation; the universal uncertainty and timidity that had seized upon all minds, determined me to bring my own mission to trial. If I should be rejected and ordered out of the country, our situation would not be worse. If I should be received, my object would be gained.... I should then stand in a fair diplomatic character, waiting the result of the national deliberations, under the protection of the government, the public faith, and the national honor.[2]

> Although they named Adams minister plenipotentiary, Congress insisted he work through the French.

I could not doubt that the count de Vergennes had information of my appointment sooner than I had, and I had a thousand reasons to believe that my whole system in Holland, and even my residence in it was disagreeable to him.... His fundamental and universal principle appeared to be to keep us entirely dependent on France.[3]

> Adams chose to ignore Congress's directive. The French ambassador to the Dutch, the Duke de la Vauguyon, tried to dissuade him.

"What!," said the Duke. "Will you take the responsibility of it upon yourself?"

"Indeed, monsieur le duke, I will; and I think I alone ought to be responsible; and that no other ambassador, minister, council or court, ought to be answerable for anything concerning it."

"Are you willing to be responsible then?"

"Indeed I am, and upon my head may all the consequences of it rest."

"Are you then determined?"

"Determined, and unalterably determined I am."[4]

Becoming the "Washington of Negotiation"

In mid-July 1781, Vergennes called Adams back to Paris for a peace conference to be mediated by Russia and Austria but without recognizing America's sovereignty. Adams, suspecting he was a pawn in some larger game, haughtily rejected this "sublime machine for demolishing our independence."[5]

> I was minister plenipotentiary for making peace: minister plenipotentiary for making a treaty of commerce with Great Britain: minister plenipotentiary to their High Mightinesses the [Dutch] States general: minister plenipotentiary to his serene highness the Prince of Orange and Stadtholder: minister plenipotentiary for pledging the faith of the United States to the [European treaty for] Armed Neutrality: and what perhaps at that critical moment was of as much importance to the United States as any of those powers, I was commissioner for negociating a loan of money to the amount of ten millions of dollars, and upon this depended the support of our army at home and our ambassadors abroad.[6]

Besides his official duties, Adams had care of the boys, John Quincy and Charles—who, homesick, would return to Braintree in mid-August 1782. When Congress assigned Francis Dana to Russia without a secretary, Adams volunteered thirteen-year-old John Quincy—with anxiety about sacrificing his formal education for practical experience.

> What did the son lose by this excursion? He lost the honor of a degree in the University of Leyden, and he lost what was more precious, the benefit of four or five years study in Greek and Roman literature under Luzac and others, and in civil law under Professor Pestell, unquestionably among the greatest masters in Europe, I should be quite unable to estimate these losses in money.[7]

From October to mid-May, Adams suffered what could have been malaria[8] from "the tainted atmosphere of Amsterdam."[9] Unaware of his illness, Congress rebuked him for delayed reports: "We frequently have had the facts ... published in the newspapers a month before their arrival."[10]

To negotiate a loan of money, to sign the obligations for it, to make a thousand visits, some idle, some not idle, all necessary, to write treaties in English, and be obliged to have them translated into French and Dutch, and to reason and discuss every article to—to—to—to—to—etc. etc. etc. is too much for my patience and strength.

My correspondence with Congress and their ministers in Europe is a great deal of work; in short, I am weary, and nobody pities me. Nobody seems to know anything about me. Nobody knows that I do any thing or have any thing to do. One thing, thank God, is certain. I have planted the American standard at the Hague. There let it wave and triumph over [British ambassador] Sir Joseph Yorke and British pride. I shall look down upon the flagstaff with pleasure from the other world.

Not the declaration of American independence, not the Massachusetts Constitution, not the alliance with France, ever gave me more satisfaction or more pleasing prospects for our country than this event. It is a pledge against friends and enemies. It is an eternal barrier against all dangers from the house of Bourbon as well as a present security against England. Perhaps every imagination does not rove into futurity as much as mine, nor care so much about it.[11]

> The Dutch officially recognized Adams as a full-fledged ambassador of an independent nation, enabling loans that would total three and a half million dollars. They also signed a treaty of amity and commerce that Adams

achieved independently but for which Congress credited the French.

After our treaty was made with Holland, the Count de Vergennes ordered the French minister to announce formally to Congress, in the name of the king, that his majesty had assisted the United States in forming the connection between them and the States General of the United provinces; and his majesty received a formal note of thanks from Congress for that favor.[12]

Returning as a peace commissioner in Paris, Adams complained again to Congress about orders to work through the French:

Taking away from us, all right of judging for ourselves, and obliging us to agree to whatever the french Ministers shall advise us to, and to nothing without their consent. I never supposed this to be the intention of Congress. If I had, I never would have accepted the commission, and if I now thought it their intention, I could not continue in it. I cannot think it possible to be the design of Congress. If it is, I hereby resign my place in the Commission and request that another person may be immediately appointed in my stead.[13]

Adams's disgust deepened as he learned Vergennes had influenced Congress to impose the restriction.

February 18, 1783. I am weary, disgusted, affronted, and disappointed.... I have been injured, and my country has joined in the injury; it has basely prostituted its own honor by sacrificing mine. But the sacrifice of me was not so servile and intolerable as putting us all under guardianship. Congress surrendered their own sovereignty into the hands of a French minister. Blush! blush! ye guilty records! blush and perish! It is glory to have broken such infamous orders. Infamous, I say, for so they will be to all posterity. How can such a stain be washed out? Can we cast a veil over it and forget it.[14]

> Before Adams's return, a separate peace treaty with Britain had been secretly negotiated by Franklin and John Jay. Jay had balked until the treaty recognized America's independence. Adams felt Jay would be a staunch friend.

November 5, 1782. Mr. Jay likes Frenchmen as little as Mr. Lee and . . . says they are not a moral people; they know not what it is; he don't like any Frenchman. . . . Our allies don't play fair, he told me; they were endeavoring to deprive us of the fishery [off the Grand Banks], the western lands, and the navigation of the Mississippi; they would even bargain with the English to deprive us of them; they want to play the western lands, Mississippi, and whole Gulf of Mexico into the hands of Spain.[15]

> To his surprise, the French received Adams upon his return from Holland as a natural hero.

In Holland, I had driven the English party and the stadtholder's party before me, like clouds before the wind, and had brought that power to unite cordially with America, France, and Spain against England.[16]

> With great show of friendship, Vergennes invited Adams to be an honored guest at a dinner party in his elegant home.

He showed me into the room where were the ladies and the company. I singled out the Countess, and went up to her to make her my compliments. The Countess and all the ladies rose up; I made my respects to them all, and turned round and bowed to the rest of the company. . . . When

Becoming the "Washington of Negotiation"

dinner was served, the Count led Madame de Montmorin, and left me to conduct the Countess, who gave me her hand with extraordinary condescension, and I conducted her to table. She made me sit next to her on her right hand, and was remarkably attentive to me the whole time. The Comte, who sat opposite, was constantly calling out to me to know what I would eat, and to offer me *petits gateux*, claret and madeira, etc. etc. In short, I was never treated with half the respect at Versailles in my life.

Adams had violated Congress's instructions in treating with the Dutch independently, yet the French lauded the treaty.

In the antechamber, before dinner, some French gentlemen ... said that I had shown in Holland that Americans understand negotiation as well as war. The compliments that have been made since my arrival in France, upon my success in Holland, would be considered as a curiosity if committed to writing.... "Monsieur, vous êtes le Washington de la négociation." ["Sir, you are the Washington of negotiation."] This is the finishing stroke. It is impossible to exceed this.[17]

On the commission, Adams saw himself as the sole representative of America's integrity.

October 27, 1782. Between two as subtle spirits as any in this world, the one malicious, the other, I think honest, I shall have a delicate, a nice, a critical part to act. Franklin's cunning will be to divide us; to this end he will provoke, he will insinuate, he will intrigue, he will manoeuvre. My curiosity will at least be employed in observing his invention and his artifice.

As part of the process, doubtlessly, Adams continued writing down Franklin's stories as his own.

November 3, 1782. The present conduct of England and America resembles that of the eagle and cat. An eagle scaling over a farmer's yard, espied a creature that he thought a hare; he pounced upon him and took him up in the air; the cat seized him by the neck with her teeth, and round the body with her fore and hind claws. The eagle finding himself scratched and pressed, bids the cat let go and fall down. "No," says the cat, "I won't let go and fall. You shall stoop and set me down."[18]

> Franklin sometimes lost patience—referring to Adams as "a certain mischievous madman."[19] "I am persuaded, however, that he means well for his Country, is always an honest man, often a wise one, but sometimes, and in some things, absolutely out of his senses."[20] However, Franklin was persuaded to join in defying Congress openly.

I went out to Passy and spent the evening with Dr. Franklin.... I told him, without reserve, my opinion of the policy of [the French] Court, and the principles, wisdom, and firmness, with which Mr. Jay had conducted the [independent] negotiation in his sickness and my absence, and that I was determined to support Mr. Jay to the utmost of my power in the pursuit of the same system. The Doctor heard me patiently, but said nothing.

The first conference we had afterwards with [British agent] Oswald, in considering one point and another, Dr. Franklin turned to Mr. Jay and said, "I am of your opinion, and will go on with these gentlemen in the business without consulting [the French] Court." He has, accordingly, met us in most of our conferences, and has gone on with us in entire harmony and unanimity throughout, and has been able and useful, both by his sagacity and his reputation, in the whole negotiation.[21]

Becoming the "Washington of Negotiation"

On 21 January 1783, they signed the preliminary treaty.

Thus drops the curtain upon this mighty Trajedy.[22]

After John Quincy returned from Russia, Adams respected his son's reluctance to talk about the confidential mission.

I never ever asked my son any questions about the motives, designs, or objects of his mission to St. Petersburgh. If I had been weak enough to ask, he would have been wise enough to be silent.[23]

He dreaded idleness as Congress left him virtually a private citizen without portfolio.

The total idleness, the perpetual uncertainty we are in, is the most insipid and at the same time disgusting and provoking situation imaginable.... I am weary, worn, and disgusted to death. I had rather chop wood, dig ditches and make fence upon my poor little farm. Alas poor farm and poorer family, what have you lost, that your country might be free, and that others might catch fish and hunt deer and beaver at their ease.[74]

Sick in body and soul, and kept in limbo by Congress, Adams would persevere against the Franklin-Vergennes axis.

Firm as some people have been complaisant enough to suppose my temper is, I assure you it has been shaken to its foundations, and more by the fluctuating councils of Philadelphia than by anything else. When a man sees entrusted to him the most essential interests of his country, sees that they depend essentially upon him, and that he must defend them against the malice of enemies, the finesse of allies, the treachery of a colleague, you may well imagine a man does not sleep on a bed of roses. It is enough to poison the life of a man in its most secret sources.... But I am not yet however so weak as to stay in Europe with a wound upon my honour.... I will not be horse jockeyed. At least, if I am, De Vergennes and Franklin shall not be the jockies.[25]

> Adams had been suffering nervous debility—"fidgets"— and pain for the past twenty months:

Sharp fiery humours which break out in the back of my neck and in other parts of me and plague me as much as the uncertainty in which I am in of my future destination.[26]

> Again, he blamed "vain, ambitious, and despotic" Vergennes along with unindicted arch-villain Franklin.

We have had to encounter another character equally selfish and interested, equally vain and ambitious, more jealous and envious, and more false and deceitful, I mean Dr. Franklin.... His whole life has been one continued insult to good manners and to decency.... I never know when he speaks the truth, and when not.... As if he had been conscious of the laziness, inactivity and real insignificance of his advanced age, he has considered every American minister, who has come to Europe, as his natural enemy.... I am persuaded he will remain as long as he lives, the Demon of Discord among our ministers, and the curse and scourge of our foreign affairs.[27]

> In October, with the definitive peace treaty signed, Adams sought to recover his broken health in English curative waters at Bath. He and John Quincy stopped for sightseeing in London. In contrast to their arrival at Bordeaux, here everyone knew his name.

I found myself in a street which was marked John's Street. The postilion turned a corner, and I was in Adam's Street. He turned another corner, and I was in John Adam's

Becoming the "Washington of Negotiation"

Street! I thought, "Surely we are arrived in Fairy Land. How can all this be? ..." I inquired of Mr. Osborne, our landlord, about the oddity of meeting my own name in all the streets about his house. I was informed that the Adelphi Hotel and all the streets and buildings about it had been planned and executed by two architects by the name of Adams [Adam]. ... The elder brother, John Adams had been permitted to give his own name to all the streets he had erected.[28]

> The painter Benjamin West arranged for them to visit Buckingham Palace. Pleased that the King's taste seemed as simple as his own, "without the smallest affectation," Adams felt even more at home in the library.

I wished for a week's time, but had but a few hours. The books were in perfect order, elegant in their editions, paper, binding, etc., but gaudy and extravagant in nothing. They were chosen with perfect taste and judgment; every book that a king ought to have always at hand, and so far as I could examine and could be supposed capable of judging, none other.

> Another American painter, John Singleton Copley, arranged for them to attend the King's speech with a pass from Chief Justice John Murray, Lord Mansfield—whom Adams had long admired for legal "learning, talents, and eloquence" but whose politics he detested.

Standing in the lobby of the House of Lords, surrounded by a hundred of the first people of the kingdom, Sir Francis Molineux, the gentleman usher of the black rod, appeared suddenly in the room with his long staff, and roared out, with a very loud voice: "Where is Mr. Adams, Lord Mansfield's friend?" I frankly avowed myself Lord Mansfield's friend, and was politely conducted by Sir Francis to my place.

A gentleman said to me the next day: "How short a time has passed since I heard that same Lord Mansfield say, in that same House of Lords, 'My Lords, if you do not kill him, he will kill you.'" Mr. West said to me this was one of the finest finishings in the picture of American Independence.[29]

> In bitter December, to save America's credit, Adams had to give up sightseeing for a perilous return to Amsterdam bankers. He and John Quincy spent three days on the "tremulous, undulating, turbulent" waves. On an island, after walking four miles through ice and snow, they rode a seatless wagon a dozen miles to the nearest iceboat on runners.

> The men broke away the thin ice forward, and rowed the boat in the water till she came to a place again strong enough to bear, when all must disembark again, and march men and boat upon the ice. How many times we were obliged to embark and disembark, in the course of the voyage, I know not, but we were all day and till quite night in making the passage. The weather was cold; we were all frequently wet; I was chilled to the heart, and looked, I suppose, as I felt, a withered old worn-out carcase. Our polite skipper frequently eyed me, and said he pitied the old man. When we got ashore, he said he must come and take the old man by the hand and wish him a safe journey to the Hague....
> I had ridden on horseback often to congress, over roads and across ferries, of which the present generation have no idea; and once, in 1777, in the dead of winter, from Braintree to Baltimore, five hundred miles, upon a trotting horse.... I had been three days in the Gulf Stream, in 1778, in a furious hurricane and a storm of thunder and lightning, which struck one of our men upon deck and cracked our

Becoming the "Washington of Negotiation"

mainmast.... I had crossed the Atlantic, in 1779, in a leaky ship, with perhaps four hundred men on board, who were scarcely able, with two large pumps going all the twenty-four hours, to keep water from filling the hold, in hourly danger, for twenty days together, of foundering at sea. I had passed the mountains in Spain, in the winter, among ice and snow, partly on mule-back and partly on foot; yet I never suffered so much in any of these situations as in that jaunt from Bath to Amsterdam in January 1784. Nor did any of those adventures ever do such lasting injuries to my health. I never got over it till my return home, in 1788.[30]

> It helped his health immeasurably when, with the commissioners now authorized to seek other treaties, he urged Abigail Adams to join him in Paris.

Come to Europe with Abby as soon as possible, and satisfy your curiosity, and improve your taste by viewing these magnificent scenes. Go to the play. See the paintings and buildings. Visit the manufactures for a few months.... I cannot be happy or tolerable without you.[31]

> In July, he loitered in London awaiting their ship. Forced to return to the Hague, he left John Quincy—now his secretary—to meet them. After Abigail Adams wrote him of their safe arrival, he rejoiced.

Your letter of the 23rd has made me the happiest man upon earth. I am twenty years younger than I was yesterday.[32]

Eighteen-year-old Abby memorialized the exciting reunion with a father whose virtues she had been "taught to fear" but who revealed "a thousand traits of softness, delicacy, and sensibility."[33]

London, August 7, 1784. At 12, returned to our own apartments; when I entered, I saw upon the table a hat with two books in it; every thing around appeared altered, without my knowing in what particular. I went into my own room, the things were moved; I looked around—

"Has mamma received letters that have determined her departure?— When does she go?— Why are these things moved?" All in a breath to Esther [the maid].

"No, ma'm, she has received no letter, but goes to-morrow morning."

"Why is all this appearance of strangeness?— Whose hat is that in the other room?— Whose trunk is this?— Whose sword and cane?—

"It is my father's!" said I "Where is he?"

"In the room above."

Up I flew, and to his chamber, where he was lying down. He raised himself upon my knocking softly at the door, and received me with all the tenderness of an affectionate parent after so long an absence."[34]

9

IMPLEMENTING INDEPENDENCE

1783–1788

The Adamses rented a sumptuous house at Auteuil for eight months of exciting Parisian life until John Adams was named the first ambassador to Britain. He would persevere against the influence of old adversaries. Congress, France, Britain, and Dutch bankers harassed him, and Dickinson's Articles of Confederation frustrated his mission. Franklin's similar plan for France angered him to write a popular three-volume defense of more balanced government. Adams would come home in glory, in contrast to the dismal era that began when he himself suggested an ambassador to the Court of Saint James.

I make no scruple nor hesitation to advise that a Minister may be sent, nor will I be intimidated from giving this advice by any apprehension that I shall be suspected of a design or desire of going to England myself. Whoever goes will neither find it a lucrative or a pleasant employment, nor will he be envied by me. . . . It is my desire to return home, at the expiration of the term of the present commissions.[1]

Unknown to Adams, Congress had already appointed him to the post—though faulting his "vanity" (to which he reacted, "I should be more vain than I am if I pretended to be at all times destitute of vanity").² Meanwhile, he tutored John Quincy who, at eighteen, returned to Harvard.

In the course of the last year, instead of playing cards like the fashionable world, I have spent my evenings with him [John Quincy]. We went with some accuracy through the Geometry in the *Praeceptor*, the eight books of Simpson's *Euclid* in Latin and compared it problem by problem and theorem by theorem with Le Père Dechâlles in french.

We went through plain Trigonometry and plain sailing, Fenning's *Algebra*, and the decimal fractions, arithmetical and geometrical proportions, and the conic sections in Ward's *Mathematicks*. . . . But alas it is thirty years since I thought of Mathematics, and I found I had lost the little I once knew, especially of these higher branches of Geometry, so he is as yet but a smatterer like his father. . . . He is studious enough and emulous enough, and when he comes to mix with his new friends and young companions he will make his way well enough.³

> Ambassador Adams arrived at Westminster on 25 May 1785, ill at ease and still wary of British intrigue.

They were fully determined, to receive me in all respects like all the other foreign Ministers. This, I believe is true. But we must be cautious what consequences we draw from it. It by no means follows, that they are determined to do, what their honour and their public faith, obliges them to do according to our ideas of their obligations.⁴

> The British would not hear of a commercial treaty, claiming that the Articles of Confederation required treating with each state separately. But on 1 June, King George III officially received Adams. As at the French court, he would be awed.

Implementing Independence

While I stood in the [antechamber] where it seems all ministers stand upon such occasions, always attended by the masters of ceremonies, the room very full of ministers of state, lords and bishops and all sorts of courtiers, as well as the next room which is the King's bed-chamber, you may well suppose that I was the focus of all eyes. I was relieved however from the embarrassment of it by the Swedish and Dutch ministers, who came to me and entertained me in a very agreeable conversation during the whole time. Some other gentlemen whom I had seen before, came to make their compliments to me, until the Marquis of Carmarthen returned and desired me to go with him to his Majesty.

> Proverbs 22:29 promised that "a man diligent in his business" would stand before kings. Adams had stood before Louis XVI of France and Willem V of the Netherlands. Now in blue silk suit and little bag wig, he stood before George III of England to whom he had once pledged fealty.

I was left with his Majesty and the Secretary of State alone. I made the three reverences, one at the door, another about half way and the third before the Presence, according to the usage established at this and all northern courts of Europe, and then addressed myself to his Majesty....

"I think myself more fortunate than all my fellow citizens in having the distinguished honor to be the first to stand in your Majesty's royal presence in a diplomatic character, and I shall esteem myself the happiest of men if I can be instrumental in recommending my country more and more to your Majesty's royal benevolence and of restoring an entire esteem, confidence and affection, or in better words, the old good nature and the old good humour between people who, tho' separated by an ocean and under different governments, have the same language, a similar religion and kindred blood. I beg your Majesty's permission to add, that altho' I have some time before been entrusted by my country, it was never my whole life in a manner so agreeable to myself."

The King listened to every word I said with dignity but with an apparent emotion—whether it was the nature of the interview or whether it was my visible agitation, for I felt more than I did or could express, that touched him I cannot say—but he was much affected and answered me with more tremor than I had spoken with, and said:

"Sir—The circumstances of this audience are so extraordinary, the language you have now held is so extremely proper and the feelings you have discovered [revealed] so justly adapted to the occasion, that I must say that I not only receive with pleasure the assurance of the friendly dispositions of the United States, but that I am very glad the choice has fallen upon you to be their Minister. I wish you, sir, to believe and that it may be understood in America, that I have done nothing in the late contest, but what I thought myself indispensably bound to do, by the duty which I owed to my People.

"I will be very frank with you. I was the last to consent to the separation, but the separation having been made and having become inevitable, I have always said, as I say now, that I would be the first to meet the friendship of the United States as an independent power. The moment I see such sentiments and language as yours prevail, and a disposition to give to this country the preference, that moment I shall say, 'Let the circumstances of language, religion and blood have their natural and full effect.'"

> Eyewitness Brook Watson reported that Adams "not a little confused . . . replied not a word."[5]

I dare not say that these were the King's precise words,

Implementing Independence

and it is even possible that I may have in some particular mistaken his meaning; for altho his pronunciation is as distinct as I ever heard, he hesitated sometimes [in mid-sentence] ... He was indeed much affected and I confess I was not less so, and therefore I cannot be certain that I was so cool and attentive, heard so clearly and understood so perfectly as to be confident of all his words or sense.

> Adams felt that the King's attempt at geniality diminished the dignity of the occasion.

The King then asked me whether I came last from France, and upon my answering in the affirmative, he put on an air of familiarity and smiling or rather laughing said, "There is an opinion among some people that you are not the most attached of all your countrymen to the manners of France."

I was surprized at this because I thought it an indiscretion and a departure from the dignity. I was a little embarrassed but determined not to deny the truth on one hand, nor leave him to infer from it any attachment to England on the other.

I threw off as much gravity as I could and assumed an air of gaiety and a tone of decision as far as was decent, and said, "That opinion, Sir, is not mistaken, I must avow to your Majesty, I have no attachment but to my own Country."

The King replied as quick as lightning, "An honest man will never have any other."[6]

> For the next three years, the Adamses put up with London's constant clatter of cobblestones, servants extorting tips, pickpockets pinching purses, and biting dampness that necessitated winter underwear during the spring.[7] Of the Court, Abigail Adams said, "I seldom meet

with characters so innofensive as my hens and chickings, or minds so well improved as my garden."⁸ In diplomatic circles, Adams occasionally found due respect.

One of the foreign ambassadors said to me, "You have been often in England."

"Never, but once in November and December, 1783."

"You have relations in England, no doubt."

"None at all."

"None? How can that be? You are of English extraction?"

"Neither my father or mother, grandfather or grandmother, great grandfather or great grandmother, nor any other relation that I know of, or care a farthing for, has been in England these one hundred and fifty years; so that you see I have not one drop of blood in my veins but what is American."

"Ay, we have seen," said he, "proof enough of that." This flattered me, no doubt, and I was vain enough to be pleased with it.⁹

> On 16 February 1786, Adams's personal diplomacy eased Barbary States attacks on American shipping. Hearing that Tripoli's ambassador had arrived, he stopped by, "so late that there was no suspicion of his being visible,"¹⁰ but the ambassador appeared.

The Ambassador was announced at home and ready to receive me. I was received in state. Two great chairs before the fire, one of which was destined for me, the other for his Excellency. Two secretaries of legation, men of no small consequence standing upright in the middle of the room, without daring to sit, during the whole time I was there, and whether they are not yet upright upon their legs I know not.

Implementing Independence

Now commenced the difficulty. His Excellency speaks scarcely a word of any European language, except Italian and Lingua Franca, in which . . . I have small pretensions. He began soon to ask me questions about America and her tobacco, and I was surprized to find that with a pittance of Italian and a few French words which he understands, we could so well understand each other.

"We make tobacco in Tripoli," said his Excellency, "but it is too strong. Your American tobacco is better."

By this time, one of his secretaries or *upper servants* brought two pipes ready filled and lighted. The longest was offered me; the other to his Excellency. It is long since I took a pipe but as it would be unpardonable to be wanting in politeness in so ceremonious an interview, I took the pipe with great complacency, placed the bowl upon the carpet, for the stem was fit for a walking cane, and I believe more than two yards in length, and smoaked in aweful pomp, reciprocating whiff for whiff with his Excellency, untill coffee was brought in.

His Excellency took a cup, after I had taken one, and alternately sipped at his coffee and whiffed at his tobacco, and I wished he would take a pinch in turn from his snuff box for variety; and I followed the example with such exactness and solemnity that the two secretaries appeared in raptures and the superiour of them who speaks a few words of French cryed out in extacy, "Monsieur votes etes un Turk."[Sir, you are a real Turk!][11]

> These droll civilities out of the way, the Ambassador offered a peace so promising that Adams called Jefferson to London. Both found nothing would ever be accomplished, obstructed by British hostility, Congressional inertia, and the Articles of Confederation.
>
> I find myself at the end of my tether—no step that I

113

can take—no language I can hold will do any good or indeed much harm. It is congress and the legislatures of the States, who must deliberate and act.[12]

The States will never think of sending separate ambassadors, or of authorizing directly those appointed by congress. The idea of thirteen plenipotentiaries meeting together in a congress at every court in Europe, each with a full power and distinct instructions from his State, presents to view such a picture of confusion, altercation, expense, and endless delay, as must convince every man of its impracticability. . . .

It is a long time that Congress have appeared to be aware of these obstructions in the way of our prosperity; but it does not yet appear that the States have been sufficiently attentive to them to remove them. It is not to be supposed that Congress will ever frame a treaty of commerce with any foreign power, which shall be unequal and partial among the States, or oppressive upon any one of them; and it is very clear, from the situation and circumstances of the country, that no such treaty can ever be carried into execution or last long.[13]

> Adams countered Franklin's single-legislature model that was being proposed for a new French parliament by writing *Defence of the Constitutions of the United States*. The first volume, published in Philadelphia in February 1787, had a major influence on delegates to the Federal Convention.

In justice to myself . . . it was not the miserable vanity of justifying my own work, or eclipsing the glory of Mr. Franklin's, that induced me to write. . . . Every western wind brought us news of town and county meetings in Massachusetts, adopting [Franklin's] ideas, condemning my [Massachusetts] Constitution, reprobating the office of governor

Implementing Independence

and the assembly of the Senate as expensive, useless, and pernicious, and not only proposing to toss them off, but rising in rebellion against them.

In this situation I was determined ... to show to the world that neither my sentiments nor actions should have any share in countenancing or encouraging any such pernicious, destructive, and fatal schemes. In this view I wrote my defence of the American Constitutions. I had only the Massachusetts Constitution in view, and such others as agreed with it in the distribution of the legislative power into three branches, in separating the executive from the legislative power, and the judiciary power from both.

These three volumes had no relation to the Constitution of the United States. That was not in existence, and I scarcely knew that such a thing was in contemplation till I received it at the moment my third volume was about to issue from the press.[14]

The manual exercise of writing was painful and distressing to me, almost like a blow on the elbow or the knee; my style was habitually negligent, unstudied, unpolished; I should make enemies of all the French patriots, the Dutch patriots, the English republicans, dissenters, reformers, call them what you will; and, what came nearer home to my bosom than all the rest, I knew I should give offence to many, if not all, of my best friends in America, and, very probably, destroy all the little popularity I ever had in a country where popularity had more omnipotence than the British parliament assumed.[15]

> With arguments based on history and on human nature, Adams showed the perils of a raw democracy versus the benefits of a balanced government resilient against endemic human error.

Popularity was never my mistress, nor was I ever, or

shall I ever be a popular man. This book will make me unpopular. But one thing I know a man must be sensible of the errors of the people, and upon his guard against them, and must run the risque of their displeasure sometimes, or he will never do them any good in the long run.[16]

April 19, Wednesday, 1786. This is the anniversary of the battle of Lexington, and of my reception at the Hague by their High Mightinesses. This last event is considered by the historians and other writers and politicians of England and France as of no consequence; and Congress and the citizens of the United States concur with them in sentiment.[17]

> Adams found relief in touring England with his family and in the June wedding of Abby at seventeen to the legation secretary William Stephen Smith.

I have given my daughter to Colonel Smith, a man of merit formed in the school of his country's afflictions. I shall want her company, in my old age, but the conveniences of parents are not the principal points to be consulted in the marriages of children.[18]

> In March 1787, as Abby had her first child, Adams projected his own sense of duty and sent Smith (as if he were John Quincy) on a diplomatic mission to Portugal.

You will have, in this journey a great opportunity of perfecting yourself in French, and of improving yourself in Spanish and the Portugese, which is but a dialect of the Spanish, and in the Italian. . . . I know very well that the situation of your family, as well as your attention to the public service, will be motives sufficient to induce you to lose no time unnecessarily.[19]

> Adams himself, worn down by Britons' dogged insults to

Implementing Independence

the honor and dignity of the United States, confided to Jefferson that he would go home and, at forty-two as he had at twenty-two, go with the flow of circumstance.

Congress cannot, consistently with their own honor and dignity, renew my commission to this Court; and I assure you, I should hold it inconsistent with my own honor and dignity, little as that may be, that, if it were possible for congress to forget theirs, I would not forget mine, but send their commission back to them, unless a minister were sent from his Britannic Majesty to Congress. As to a residence in Holland, that climate is so destructive to my health, that I could never bear it; and I am sure it would be fatal to her, on whom depends all the satisfaction that I have in life. . . .

For a man who has been for thirty years rolling like a stone, never three years in the same place, it is no very pleasant speculation to cross the seas, with a family, in a state of uncertainty what is to be his fate, what reception he shall meet at home, whether he shall settle down in private life to his plough, or push into the turbulent scenes of sedition and tumult; whether he be sent to congress, or a convention, or God knows what. If it lay in my power, I would take a vow to retire to my little turnip-yard, and never again quit it. I feel very often a violent disposition to take some resolution, and swear to it; but upon the whole, it is best to preserve my liberty to do as I please, according to circumstances.[20]

With similar comments to John Jay, Adams proposed a new activity.

The convention of Philadelphia is composed of heroes, sages, and demigods, to be sure, who want no assistance from me in forming the best possible plan; but they may have occasion for underlaborers, to make it accepted by the people, or, at least, to make them unanimous in it and contented with it. One of these underworkmen, in a cool retreat, it shall be my ambition to become.[21]

> At year's end, Congress voted to allow John Adams to go home—with thanks for ten years of "patriotism, perseverance, integrity, and diligence."[22] But they were late with the official notice to British and Dutch courts, leaving Adams in limbo, fuming.

There is no alternative now left for me; home I must go, and leave all Europe to conjecture that I have given offence in Holland; and, in England, that I have misbehaved abroad, though my conduct has been approved at home. When the public shall hear that I have gone home, without taking leave, there will be no end of criticism, conjectures, and reflections.[23]

> Then, in February 1788, just as the Adamses were ready to sail, Jefferson asked for help negotiating loans from speculators to cover debts due at Amsterdam. Adams commiserated and complied.

I know not how to express to you the sense I have of the disingenuousness of this plot. The difficulty of selling the obligations, I believe to be mere pretence; and indeed the whole appears to me to be a concerted fiction.... I feel no vanity in saying that this project never would have been suggested, if it had not been known that I was recalled.... Damned and teazed as you will be, all your philosophy will be wanting to support you. But be not discouraged. I have been constantly vexed with such terrible complaints, and frightened with such long faces, these ten years.

Depend upon it, the Amsterdamers love money too well to execute their threats. They expect to get too much by American credit, to destroy it.[24]

Implementing Independence

He combined the business of banking with the pleasure of taking formal leave of the Dutch bankers and court.

> I thought myself dead ... as a public man: but I think I shall be forced, after my decease, to open an additional loan. At least this is Mr. Jefferson's opinion.[25]

The Adamses embarked, 30 March, on stormy seas. "I hope and pray," sighed Abigail Adams, "I may never again be left to go to sea: of all places, it is the most disagreeable, such sameness, and such a tossing to and fro."[26] They docked at Boston on a cool, breezy mid-June day with cannons saluting, bells ringing, several thousand cheering on the pier, and the coach and four bouncing over cobblestones to Governor Hancock's mansion, where they spent the night. The next day, separately and secretly, Abigail and John Adams went home.[27] Writing to Abby, now on Long Island, he devalued his popularity and asserted his pride in public service as its own reward.

> You may be anxious, too, to know what is to become of me. At my age [53] this ought not to be a question; but it is. I will tell you, my dear child, in strict confidence, that it appears to me that your father does not stand very high in the esteem, admiration, or respect of his country, or any part of it. In the course of a long absence his character has been lost, and he has got quite out of circulation. The public judgment, the public heart, and the public voice, seem to have decreed to others every public office that he can accept of with consistency, or honour, or reputation; and no other alternative is left for him, but private life at home, or to go again abroad. The latter is the worst of the two; but you may depend upon it, you will hear of him on a trading voyage to the East Indies, or to Surrinam, or Essequibo, before you will hear of his descending as a public man beneath himself.[28]

10

SUCCEEDING WASHINGTON

1788–1801

John Adams deserved a rest. Despite newfound celebrity, he turned down a seat in the Senate. He hoped to make up for the years away from his family—a sacrifice that he rationalized had been for their sake.

I must study politics and war, that my sons may have liberty to study mathematics and philosophy. My sons ought to study mathematics and philosophy, geography, natural history and naval architecture, navigation, commerce, and agriculture, in order to give their children a right to study painting, poetry, music, architecture, statuary, tapestry, and porcelain.[1]

While their parents were abroad, the boys had lived with a maternal aunt. Thomas was sixteen; Charles seventeen. John Quincy at twenty-one had already commenced a career in diplomacy.

The oldest has given decided proofs of great talents, and there is not a youth of his age whose reputation is higher for abilities, or whose character is fairer in point of morals or conduct. The youngest is as fine a youth as either of the three, if a spice of fun in his composition should not lead him astray. Charles wins the heart, as usual, and is the most of a gentleman of them all.²

They are regular in their manners and studies, and give me so much satisfaction as to increase the regret I feel at the remembrance of how much of their interests I have been obliged to sacrifice to the public service.³

> For six hundred pounds, the Adamses bought a larger Braintree house, suited to the entertainments expected of a celebrity. He still had the farm for recreation.

I found my estate, in consequence of a total neglect and inattention on my part . . . was falling to decay, and in so much disorder as to require my whole attention to repair it. . . . It is not large, in the first place. It is but the farm of a patriot. But there are in it two or three spots, from whence are to be seen some of the most beautiful prospects in the world.⁴

I have indeed enjoyed a delightful rest, tho my mind has been constantly employed with my private and domestic affairs, which by a negligence of fifteen years were in such disorder, as would require several years to rectify. The period from the 17 June, 1788, to this 2d of March, 1789, has been the sweetest morsel of my life, and I despair of ever tasting such another. This delightful retreat, humble as it is, I shall quit with great regret. There never was and never will be found for me, an office in public life, that will furnish the entertainment and refreshment of the mountain, the meadow and the stream.⁵

> Adams could not subsist on farming, and returning to law would have ignored popular demand that he run for office in the new government. Still, he had reservations about popular elections.

Elections . . . to offices which are a great object of ambition,

Succeeding Washington

I look at with terror. Experiments of this kind have been so often tried, and so universally found productive of horrors, that there is great reason to dread them. . . .[6] If the time should come when corruption shall be added to intrigue and maneuver in elections, and produce civil war, then in my opinion, chance will be better than choice for all but the House of Representatives.[7]

> By the close of 1788, Adams was the popular choice for vice president.[8] Hamilton maneuvered electoral voting so that Washington won sixty-eight and Adams merely thirty-four—a total, said Adams, "that made it a disgrace."[9] Yet he would sacrifice dignity to duty.

For "eminence" I care nothing; for though I pretend not to be exempt from ambition, or any other human passion, I have been convinced from my infancy and have been confirmed every year and day of my life, that the mechanic and peasant are happier than any nobleman, or magistrate, or king, and that the higher a man rises, if he has any sense of duty, the more anxious he must be.[10]

> Restricted from debate, Adams could do little more than preside over a recalcitrant Senate. He never missed a day. He wore his ambassador's blue velvet suit, bag wig, and sword. The Senate lampooned him to his face.[11]

It may be found easier to give authority, than to yield obedience.[12]

> Trying to reconcile the rhetoric of democracy to the ceremonies of state, Adams raised the question of titles. Senators mocked him as "His Rotundity"[13] and taunted him as a monarchist. He held out for dignity.

[I] asked in what form I should address him; whether I should say, "Mr. Washington," "Mr. President," "Sir," "May it please your Excellency," or what else? I observed that it had been common while he commanded the army to call him "His Excellency," but I was free to own it would appear to me better to give him no title but "Sir" or "Mr. President," than to put him on a level with a governor of Bermuda, or one of his ambassadors, or a governor of any one of our States.[14]

> Adams rejected the abstract notion of such equality.

By the law of nature, all men are men, and not angels—men, and not lions—men, and not whales—men, and not eagles—that is, they are all of the same species; and this is the most that the equality of nature amounts to.[15]

> Adams published "Discourses on Davila" in the *Gazette of the United States* (serially from 28 April 1790 to 27 April 1791), concluding that men acted from a basic need for recognition. Suggesting that hereditary rulers as models would be good for revolutionary France opened him to charges of "aristocrat" and "monarchist."

This dull, heavy volume still excites the wonder of its author,—first, that he could find, amidst the constant scenes of business and dissipation in which he was enveloped, time to write it; secondly, that he had the courage to oppose and publish his own opinions to the universal opinion of America, and, indeed, of all mankind. Not one man in America then believed him.... The work, however, powerfully operated to destroy his popularity. It was urged as full proof, that he was an advocate for monarchy, and laboring to introduce a hereditary president in America.[16]

> When Jefferson's anonymous preface to Paine's *Rights of Man* attacked the "Discourses" as political heresy, John Quincy Adams attacked Jefferson by name in the newspapers. "Thus," said Jefferson, "were our names thrown on

the public stage as public antagonists."[17] At first, John Adams pretended disdain.

> My head I thank God is not easily diverted from its views nor my heart from its resolutions; and therefore neither Paine nor his Godfather [i.e., Jefferson] will much affect me, and I believe they will affect the Public as little. It only grieves me that a character who stood so high is so much lowered in the public esteem.[18]

But the wound would not heal.

> The question every where was, "What heresies are intended by the Secretary of State?" The answer in the newspapers was, "The Vice President's notion of a limited monarchy, an hereditary government of kings and lords, with only elective commons." Emboldened by these murmurs, soon after appeared the paragraphs of an unprincipled libeller in the New Haven *Gazette*, carefully reprinted in the papers of New York, Boston and Philadelphia, holding up the Vice President to the ridicule of the world, for his meanness, and to their detestation for wishing to subjugate the people to a few nobles....
>
> My unpolished writings, although they have been read by a sufficient number of persons to have assisted in crushing the insurrection of Massachusetts, in the formation of the new constitutions of Pensilvania, Georgia and South Carolina and in procuring the assent of all the States to the new national Constitution, yet they have not been read by great numbers. Of the few who have taken the pains to read them, some have misunderstood them and others have willfully misrepresented them, and these misunderstandings and misrepresentations have been made the pretence for overwhelming me with floods and whirlwinds of tempestuous abuse, unexampled in the history of this country.[19]

Despite the abuse, Adams won reelection with a respectable seventy-seven electoral votes. Excluded from the Cabinet, he was spared the political infighting that divided the nation into Hamiltonian Federalists and Jeffersonian Democratic-Republicans. He resigned himself to circumstances.

—I know not how it is, but in proportion as dangers [from revolutionary France] threaten the public, I grow calm. I am very apprehensive that a desperate anti-federal party [supporting the French] will provoke all Europe by their insolence. But my country has in its wisdom contrived for me the most insignificant office that ever the invention of man contrived or his imagination conceived. And as I can do neither good nor evil, I must be borne away by others, and meet the common fate.[20]

—I, for my part, am wearied to death with *ennui*. Obliged to be punctual in my habits, confined to my seat, as in a prison, to see nothing done, to hear nothing said, and to say and do nothing. O, that my rocks were here within a mile or two, and my little habitation, and pretty little wife above all. Ah, I fear that some fault unknown has brought upon me such punishments, to be separated both when we were too young and when we are too old.[21]

—Such is the critical state of our public affairs, and I daily hear such doctrines advanced and supported by almost and sometimes quite one half of the senate, that I shall not prevail on myself to abandon my post.... I have not been absent a day. It is, to be sure, a punishment to hear other men talk five hours every day, and not be at liberty to talk at all myself, especially as more than half I hear appears to me very young, inconsiderate,and inexperienced.[22]

—You would admire to see with what serenity and in-

Succeeding Washington

trepidity I commonly sit and hear.... If dignity consists in total insensibility, I believe my countenance has it.[23]
—I shall say nothing of public affairs, because the least said is soonest mended.[24]

> When in a sardonic mood, Adams could joke about the venom and the volume of radical attacks that would lead Washington to retire.

Our anti-federal scribblers are so fond of rotations [in office] that they seem disposed to remove their abuse from me to the President . . . for his drawing rooms, levees, declining to accept invitations to dinners and tea parties. . . . I have held the office of Libelee General long enough. The burden of it ought to be participated and equalized according to modern republican principles.[25]

> With his customary sense of self-doubt, Adams would have been happy to retire with Washington, satisfied with either Republican Jefferson or Federalist John Jay as president.

I love my country too well to shrink from danger in her service, provided I have a reasonable prospect of being able to serve her honor and advantage. But if I have reason to think that I have either a want of abilities or of public confidence to such a degree as to be able to support the government in a higher station, I ought to decline it. But in that case, I ought not to serve in my present place under another, especially if that other should entertain sentiments so opposite to mine as to endanger the peace of the nation.[26]

> After Washington made it clear that Adams was the "heir apparent," Adams once more reluctantly accepted destiny.

—I have a pious and a philosophical resignation to the

voice of the people in this case, which is the voice of God. I have no very ardent desire to be the butt of party malevolence. Having tasted of that cup, I find it bitter, nauseous, and unwholesome.[27]

—I am weary of the game, yet I don't know how I could live out of it. I don't love slight, neglect, contempt, disgrace, nor insult, more than others. Yet I believe I have firmness of mind enough to bear it like a man, a hero, and a philosopher. I might groan like Achilles, and roll from side to side abed sometimes, at the ignorance, folly, injustice and ingratitude of the world, but I should be resigned, and become more easy and cheerful.[28]

—I feel no ill feelings or faint misgivings. I have not the smallest dread of private life nor of public. If private life is to be my portion, my farm and my pen shall employ the rest of my days.[29]

> The reluctant candidate spent the summer at "Peacefield" (named for the peace treaty) reading, writing, and farming as a sixty-year-old country squire.

August 4, 1796. Thursday. Of all the summers of my life, this has been the freest from care, anxiety, and vexation to me, the sickness of Mrs. A. excepted. My health has been better, the season fruitful, my farm was well conducted. Alas! what may happen to reverse all this? But it is folly to anticipate evils, and madness to create imaginary ones.[30]

> Adams won seventy-one electoral votes against Jefferson's sixty-eight (making Jefferson vice president) and merely fifty-nine for Hamilton's candidate, C.C. Pinckney. Once again, he saw himself as a victim of necessity.

To myself, personally, "my election" might be a matter of indifference or rather of aversion. Had Mr. Jay, or some others, been in question, it might have less mortified my vanity, and infinitely less alarmed my apprehensions for the public. But to see such a character as Jefferson, and much more such an unknown being as Pinckney, brought over my head, and trampling on the bellies of hundreds of other men infinitely his superiors in talents, services, and reputation, filled me with apprehensions for the safety of us all. It demonstrated to me that, if the project succeeded, our Constitution could not have lasted four years.[31]

> Adams worried about setting up a household in Philadelphia as presidential as Washington's had been.

Our prospects appear every day worse and worse. House rent at 2700 dollars a year, 1500 dollars for a carriage, 1000 for a pair of horses, all the glasses, ornaments, kitchen furniture, the best chairs, settees, plateaus, etc., all to purchase, all the china, delph and wedgewood, glass and crockery of every sort to purchase, and not a farthing probably will the House of Representatives allow, though the Senate have voted a small addition. All the linen besides. I shall not pretend to keep more than one pair of horses for a carriage, and one for a saddle. Secretaries, servants, wood, charities, which are demanded as rights, and the million dittoes present such a prospect as is enough to disgust any one.... We cannot go back. We must stand our ground as long as we can.[32]

> At the inauguration General Washington, dressed as an ordinary citizen, stood aside for him. Adams told Abigail Adams, who was ailing at home, how deeply the ceremony moved him.

A solemn scene it was, indeed; and it was made more affecting to me by the presence of the General, whose countenance was as serene and unclouded as the day. He seemed to me to enjoy a triumph over me. Methought I heard him say: "Ay! I am fairly out, and you fairly in! See which of us will be happiest."

When the ceremony was over, he came and made me a visit, and cordially congratulated me, and wished my administration might be happy, successful, and honorable.

In the chamber of the House of Representatives was a multitude as great as the space could contain, and I believe scarcely a dry eye but Washington's. The sight of the sun setting full orbed, and another rising, though less splendid, was a novelty. Chief Justice [Oliver] Ellsworth administered the oath, and with great energy....

> Adams's inaugural address—with one sentence longer than a thousand words—reassured the people that he would not restore monarchy but trust the "honor, spirit, and resources of the American people" to reach their high destinies.

I had not slept well the night before, and did not sleep well the night after. I was unwell, and did not know whether I should get through or not. I did, however. How the business was received, I know not, only I have been told that ... "taken altogether, it was the sublimest thing ever exhibited in America."[33]

> He was no George Washington, but he too aimed for a strong, nonpartisan, independent presidency—despite the obligatory distractions.

I hate speeches, messages, addresses and answers, proclamations, and such affected, studied, constrained things. I hate levees and drawing rooms. I hate to speak to a thousand people to whom I have nothing to say. Yet all this I can do. But I am too old [at age sixty-one] to continue more than one, or at most more than two heats, and that is scarcely time enough to form, conduct and complete any useful system.[34]

Succeeding Washington

He retained Washington's Cabinet even though suspecting them of being under Hamilton's influence.

> When I came into office, it was my determination to make as few removals as possible—not one from personal motives, not one from party considerations. . . . If the officers of government will not support it, who will?[35]

In contrast to his earlier fumings at Hutchinson, Dickinson, Franklin, or Vergennes, Adams now quietly bided his time.

> —John Adams remains *Semper idem* [always the same], both Federalist and Republican in every rational and intelligible sense of both those words.[36]
>
> —If there ever was an "Hamilton Conspiracy" . . . its object was not "a northern confederation." Hamilton's ambition was too large for so small an aim. He aimed at commanding the whole Union, and he did not like to be shackled even with an alliance with Great Britain. . . . No! H. had wider views! If he could have made a tool of Adams as he did of Washington, he hoped to erect such a government as he pleased over the whole Union, and enter into allyance with France or England as would suit his convenience.[37]

Adams showed remarkable patience or temerity or indecision. As vicious partisan fighting flowed from the press to the streets, Adams endured "terrorism."

> Upon this subject I despair of making myself understood by posterity, by the present age, and even by you [Jefferson]. . . . You never felt the terrorism of Shays's rebellion in Massachusetts. . . . You certainly never felt the terrorism excited by Genet, in 1793, when ten thousand people in the streets of Philadelphia, day after day, threatened to drag Washington out of his house, and effect a revolution in the government, or compel it to declare war in favor of

the French revolution and against England.... I have no doubt you were fast asleep, in philosophical tranquillity, when ten thousand people, and, perhaps, many more, were parading the streets of Philadelphia ... when Market street was as full as men could stand by one another, and, even before my door; when some of my domestics, in frenzy, determined to sacrifice their lives in my defence; when all were ready to make a desperate sally among the multitude, and others were, with difficulty and danger, dragged back by the rest; when I, myself, judged it prudent and necessary to order chests of arms from the war-office to be brought through by-lanes and back-doors, determined to defend my house.[38]

> Much of the agitation had spilled over from the European conflicts that Adams had tried to avoid. The Jay Treaty favored England, so the French attacked America in the Quasi War. To restrain radical Francophiles, Adams reluctantly signed the Alien and Sedition Acts restricting civil liberties and enraging the press.

We were then at war with France. French spies then swarmed in our cities and our country; some of them were intolerably impudent, turbulent, and seditious. To check these, was the design of [the Alien] law. Was there ever a government which had not authority to defend itself against spies in its own bosom—spies of an enemy at war? This law was never executed by me in any instance.[39]

> Twenty-five suspects were arrested under the Sedition Act. President Jefferson would eventually pardon the eleven who were convicted.

The Comte de Vergennes once said to me, "Mr. Adams, the newspapers govern the world!"[40] ... If I am to judge by the newspapers and pamphlets that have been printed in

Succeeding Washington

America for twenty years past, I should think that both parties believed me the meanest villain in the world.[41]... If I had no thanks from the republicans, I had nothing but insolence and scurvility from the federalists.[42]

> Adding to his misery, Adams's mother died, his son Charles was dying slowly from alcoholism, and his wife of thirty-five years was wasting away with recurring fevers.

—[Her] sickness last summer, fall, and winter has been to me the severest trial I ever endured. Not that I am at this moment without other trials, enough for one man.[43]

—A peck of troubles in a large bundle of papers, often in a hand-writing almost illegible, comes every day.... Thousands of sea letters, Mediterranean passes, and commissions and patents to sign—no company—no society—idle, unmeaning ceremony, follies, extravagances, shiftlessness, and health sinking, for what I know, under my troubles and fatigues.[44]

> Public outrage flared as France tried to extort bribes from Adams's diplomats and attack American ships. To head national defense, Adams turned to Washington, whose insistence on enlisting Hamilton added to internal unrest. Finally, Adams invoked his treaty-making powers to negotiate a peace with France that was at once honorable abroad and popular at home—the jewel crowning his administration.

I humbled the French Directory as much as all Europe has humbled Bonaparte. I purchased navy yards.... built frigates, manned a navy, and selected officers with great anxiety and care, who perfectly protected our commerce, and gained virgin victories against the French....

I was engaged in the most earnest, sedulous, and, I must own, expensive exertions to preserve peace with the Indians, and prepare them for agriculture and civilization, through the whole of my administration. I had the inexpressible satisfaction of complete success. Not a hatchet was lifted in my time....

I finished the demarcation of limits, and settled all controversies with Spain. I made the composition with England, for all the old Virginia debts, and all the other American debts, the most snarling, angry, thorny, *scabreux* [scabrous] negotiation that ever mortal ambassador, king, prince, emperor, or president was ever plagued with....

I had complete and perfect success, and left my country at peace with all the world, upon terms consistent with the honor and interest of the United States, and with all our relations with other nations, and all our obligations by the law of nations or by treaties....

I left navy yards, fortifications, frigates, timber, naval stores, manufactories of cannon and arms, and a treasury full of five millions of dollars. This was all done step by step, against perpetual oppositions, clamors and reproaches, such as no other President ever had to encounter, and with a more feeble, divided, and incapable support than has ever fallen to the lot of any administration before or since.[45]

> Doubting that even this record would ensure reelection in 1800, Adams prepared to go gently into retirement.

The business of the office is so oppressive that I shall hardly support it two years longer ... Rivalries have been irritated to madness.... But I will not take revenge. I do not remember that I was ever vindictive in my life, though I have often been very wroth. I am not very angry now, nor much vexed or fretted.[46]

> Just before the election, Hamilton issued a thirty-page pamphlet accusing Adams of malfeasance, dividing the Federalists enough for Jefferson and Burr to win.

Succeeding Washington

All the old patriots, all the splendid talents, the long experience, both of federalists and antifederalists, must be subjected to the humiliation of seeing this dexterous gentleman [Burr] rise, like a balloon, filled with inflammable air, over their heads. And this is not the worst. What a discouragement to all virtuous exertion, and what an encouragement to party intrigue, and corruption!⁴⁷

> Adams spent his last month as president naming sixteen circuit judges under the new Judiciary Act and appointing John Marshall Chief Justice. He prayed for the new president's house and for the new city of Washington.

—May none but honest and wise men ever rule under this roof!⁴⁸

—May this territory be the residence of virtue and happiness! In this city may that piety and virtue, that wisdom and magnanimity, that constancy and self-government, which adorned the great character whose name it bears, be forever held in veneration! Here, and throughout our country, may simple manners, pure morals, and true religion flourish forever!⁴⁹

> He did not stay for the inauguration.

11

OUTLIVING ENEMIES

1801–1826

Being John Adams, he could not go gently into retirement. He would spend the next twenty-five years trying to justify having sacrificed family and fortune: "I was borne along by an irresistible sense of duty."[1] Summing up his service, he wrote about himself as "Hobby Horse."

He spent 17 years at the bar, riding circuits, getting money and a wife and children. But the 17 years flew away like the morning cloud.... Four years were then spent in Congress.... But they were gone like a dream.... Then he was ten years in Europe, on the mountain wave, over the hills and far away. But the ten years were gone he scarcely knew how.... He had then an interval of eight or nine months. Then he was eight years Vice-President, a target for the archers, a constant object of the billingsgate, scurrility, misapprehensions, misconstructions, misrepresentations, lies, and libels of all parties. These eight went away like a nauseous fog.... He was then President for 4 years. A tale told by an idiot, full of sound and fury, signifying nothing. Vanity of vanities, all was vanity![2]

In spring 1803 the Adamses came close to losing their home when their London banker crashed. John Quincy rescued them, ensuring financial security enough for John Adams to be a farmer again.

I call for my leavers and iron bars, for my chisels, drills and wedges to split rocks, and for my waggons to cart seaweed for manure upon my farm. I mount my horse and ride on the sea shore: and I walk upon Mount Wollaston and Stonyfield Hill. Notwithstanding all this I read the public papers and documents, and I cannot and will not be indifferent to the condition and prospects of my country.[3]

> The press periodically attacked Adams. He enjoyed outlasting libelers like Philadelphia's Andrew Brown, who died when his house burned down, Benjamin Bache and John Fenno, who both died of yellow fever, and Alexander Callender, who drowned.

I have often heard Dr. Franklin say that, "One of the pleasures of old age was to outlive one's enemies." ... I could swell this catalogue to much greater length by enumerating instances of individuals and parties who have been marked with signal misfortune after having been guilty of injustice and baseness to me [and title it] "An History of God's Judgments against Lyars and Libellers."[4]

> By contrast, as titles came into fashion John Adams enjoyed a new but temporary respect.

It is become fashionable to call me "The Veneerable." It makes me think of the Venerable Bede. . . . The gentlemen of the Navy Yard at Washington have lately called me the modern Nestor. I like that title much better. Pray change the title and say the venerable Washington, the venerable Jefferson, and the venerable Madison: I have worn it too long. It is become threadbare upon me. Do not however, I pray you call me [as Washington was called] the "Godlike

Outliving Enemies

Adams," "the Sainted Adams," . . . "Our Saviour on Earth and our Advocate in Heaven," "the Father of his Country," "the Founder of the American Republic," "The Founder of the American Empire," etc., etc., etc. These ascriptions belong to no man; no! nor to any twenty men; nor to any hundred men, nor to any thousand men.[5]

—Mausauleums, statues, monuments will never be erected to me.[6]

—The history of our Revolution will be one continued lye from one end to the other. The essence of the whole will be that Dr. Franklin's electrical rod smote the earth and out sprung General Washington. That Franklin electrified him with his rod—and thence forward these two conducted all the policy, negotiations, legislatures and war. These . . . lines contain the whole fable, plot, and catastrophy. If this letter should be preserved, and read a hundred years hence the reader will say, "The envy of this J. A. could not bear to think of the Truth! He ventured to scribble . . . blasphemy that he dared not speak when he lived."[7]

Adams himself played coy about contributing the "Truth."

—I write no biographies or biographical sketches; I give only hints. . . .[8]

—I could entertain you with many little trifling anecdotes, which, though familiar and vulgar, would indicate the temper, feelings, and forebodings among the people, that I cannot write.[9]

Adams would generously supply data to biographers like Jedediah Morse, and autobiographical sketches to the Boston *Patriot,* even when he found them a waste of time.

—I now think I was very idly employed in vindicating my conduct.[10]

He would not write his own history of the Revolution. At eighty, Adams blamed old age—"Sans eyes, sans hands, sans memory, sans clerks, . . . sans aids-de-camp, sans amanuensis"[11]—and his own negligence.

> Of all men who have acted a part in the great affairs of the world, I am afraid I have been the most careless and negligent in preserving papers. I must write too many things from memory, and oftentimes facts to which there is no other witness alive. The task, besides, is so extensive that I have not time left to execute it. To rummage trunks, letter books, bits of journals, and great heaps and bundles of old papers is a dreadful bondage to old age and an extinguisher of old eyes.[12]

He did, however, begin an autobiography in 1802, pleading self-defense.

> My excuse is, that having been the object of much misrepresentation, some of my Posterity may wish to see in my own hand writing a proof of the falsehood of that Mass of odious abuse of my character, with which news papers, private letters and public pamphlets and histories have been disgraced for thirty years.[13]

Off and on for seven years Adams would work on the narrative, until breaking off at the events of 1780. He was enraged by random passages in Mercy Otis Warren's three-volume *History of the Rise, Progress and Termination of the American Revolution* (1806) that he interpreted as criticizing him for vanity and ambition.

> If by "ambition" you mean a love of power or a desire of public offices, I answer, I never solicited a vote in my life for any public office. I never swerved from any principle . . . to obtain a vote. I never sacrificed a friend or betrayed a trust. I never hired scribblers to defame my rivals. I never

wrote a line of slander against my bitterest enemy, nor encouraged it in any other.... When I was finally turned out of the highest office in the nation by the arts of a Burr and a Hamilton, and by innumerable other arts... have I complained? Have I been dejected? Have I been enraged? Ask those who know me. Ambition disappointed naturally turns into revenge. It produces rage, violence, envy, malice, hatred, and perpetual projects to recover the lost consideration... I can sincerely declare that the last seven years have been the happiest of my life.[14]

> With the same sensitivity, when Massachusetts senator James Lloyd criticized his having sent peace missions to France, Adams cast aside false modesty.

I will defend my missions to France, as long as I have an eye to direct my hand, or a finger to hold my pen. They were the most disinterested and meritorious actions of my life. I reflect upon them with so much satisfaction, that I desire no other inscription over my gravestone than: "Here lies John Adams, who took upon himself the responsibility of the peace with France in the year 1800."... I was turned out of office, degraded and disgraced by my country; and I was glad of it. I felt no disgrace, because I felt no remorse....[15] I thought my duty to my country ought to prevail over every personal and party consideration.[16]

> Adams opened himself similarly in letters to Dr. Benjamin Rush, a pioneer in psychiatry, sharing memories of the Revolution and sentiments of the sort once meant for his diary and Abigail Adams.

I am very sensible that I have been negligent of [fame] to a fault, and a very great fault, too. There have been very many times in my life when I have been so agitated in my own mind as to have no consideration at all of the light in which my words, actions, and even writings would be considered by others. Indeed, I never could bring myself seriously to consider that I was a great man or of much importance or consideration in the world. The few traces that remain of me must, I believe, go down to posterity in much confusion and distraction, as my life has been passed. Enough surely of Egotism![17]

> "I feel at least forty years younger when I am writing to you," he told Rush.[18] He relished roasting such deceased enemies as Hamilton—"[that] bastard brat of a Scotch pedlar,"[19]—and Tom Paine.

[Paine's] conversation always disgusting was one day uncommonly vain, rude, and arrogant at table, and in some dispute about government he talked so much like a villain and a blockhead as to excite me to wrath, and I called him, not jocularly, but bona fide and in sober earnest, "A fool." I must confess, that to call him so to his face in my own house and at my own table was such a violation of his rights and my duties of hospitality, that I would readily ask his pardon, even at this day if his pardon was worth having.[20]

> In 1812, Adams and Jefferson reconciled after Rush relayed Adams's statement, "I always loved Jefferson, and still love him."[21] Thereafter followed lively exchanges as of old.

Sitting at my fireside with my daughter [Abby Adams] Smith, on the first of February, my servant brought me a bundle of letters and newspapers from the post office in this town; one of the first letters ... struck my eye. Reading the superscription, I instantly handed the letter to Mrs. Smith. "Is that not Mr. Jeffersons hand?"

Looking attentively at it, she answered, "It is very like it."

Opening the letter I found it, indeed, from Monticello

Outliving Enemies

in the hand and with the signature of Mr. Jefferson. But this did not much diminish my surprize. "How is it possible a letter can come from Mr. Jefferson to me in seven or eight days?" I had no expectation of an answer, thinking the distance so great and the roads so embarrassed, under two or three months.

This history would not be worth recording but for the discovery it made of a fact, very pleasing to me, viz. that the communication between us is much easier, surer and may be more frequent than I had ever believed or suspected to be possible.

> Adams then introduced the topics of aging and family that would recur regularly alongside debates on education, government, the arts, and their own roles in history.

I walk every fair day sometimes three or four miles. Ride now and then but very rarely more than ten or fifteen miles. But I have a complaint that nothing but the ground can cure, that is the palsy; a kind of paralytic affection of the nerves, which makes my hand tremble, and renders it difficult to write at all and impossible to write well.[22]

> Following Rush's death the next year, Jefferson became Adams's favorite correspondent. "Every line from you exhilarates my spirits and gives me a glow of pleasure."[23] They would correct each other about such critical events as Adams's intercepted letter that called Dickinson "a piddling genius."

It was in the month of June 1775. . . . In June 1776 my friends would not have put on long faces and lamented my imprudence. None of them would have wondered, as some of them did in 1775, that a man of forty years of age, and of considerable experience in business, and in life should have been guilty of such an indiscretion. Others would not have

143

said, "It was a premature declaration of independence," and Joseph Reed . . . would not have said to me, as he did, "I look upon the interception and publication of that letter, as an act of the providence of God, to excite the attention of the people to their real situation, and to shew them, what they must come to."[24]

> He delighted most in sharing with Jefferson views on classical literature and moral philosophy, on religion both public and private ("The ten commandments and the sermon on the mount contain my religion").[25] At age eighty-one, Adams imagined a dialogue with his seventy-three-year-old friend.

J. Would you agree to live your eighty years over again for ever?

A. . . . I own my soul would start and shrink back on itself at the prospect of an endless succession of *boules de savon* [soap bubbles], almost as much as at the certainty of annihilation. For what is human life? I can speak only for one. I have had more comfort than distress, more pleasure than pain, ten to one; nay, if you please, a hundred to one. A pretty large dose, however, of distress and pain.

> Having seen his son Charles at thirty suffer death from alcoholism, he watched his adored daughter Abby at forty-eight lose an excruciating struggle against breast cancer.

But, after all, what is human life? A vapor, a fog, a dew, a cloud, a blossom, a flower, a rose, a blade of grass, a glass bubble, a tale told by an idiot, a *boule de savon*, vanity of vanities, an eternal succession of which would terrify me almost as much as annihilation. . . .

J. Would you live over again once or forever rather than run the risk of annihilation, or of a better or worse state at or after death?

Outliving Enemies

A. Most certainly I would not.
J. How valiant you are!
A. Aye, at this moment and at all other moments of my life that I can recollect; but who can tell what will become of his bravery, when his flesh and his philosophy were not sufficient to support him in his last hours.[26]

> Adams would fall from this height of speculation to the depths of despair as Abigail Adams, at seventy-three, lingered with the typhoid fever that killed her on 28 October 1818.

The dear partner of my life for fifty four years as a wife and for many years more as a lover, now lyes in extremis, forbidden to speak or be spoken to. If human life is a bubble, no matter how soon it breaks. If it is as I firmly believe an immortal existence we ought patiently to wait the instructions of the great Teacher.[27]

> The emotional vacuum that was created by Abigail's death would in time be filled by the gaggle of grandchildren that encircled him in retirement. By this time, there were at least fourteen living in the house now being looked after by his daughter-in-law Nancy and his niece Louisa Smith.[28] With old friends Adams would compare joys of grandparenting.

—I have the start of you in age by at least ten years: but you are advanced to the rank of a Great Grandfather before me. Of 13 grand children I have two [boys], William and John Smith, and three girls, Caroline Smith [Nabby's children], Susanna and Abigail Adams [Charles's daughters] who might have made me great-grandchildren enough. But they are not likely to employ their talents very soon. They are all good boys and girls however, and are the solace of my age [seventy-seven].[29]

—[At eighty-six, I] have seven grand-children, scattered over the world, and seven more under my own roof, and eight or ten great grandchildren, one of whom is here with her mother. A great-granddaughter, and a great-grandson of the same age, three years; whose sports, capers, gambols, and droleries are diverting as any harlequins on any stage.[30]

> Jefferson's favorite granddaughter, Ellen Coolidge, found Adams, "surrounded by grandchildren exceedingly attached to him, and watching over him with great care and tenderness."[31] Neighboring girls would seek advice on love and marriage. At eighty-eight, he flirted coyly.

You have much better advisers than I can be—but I will venture [to] suggest one line. As Nature will attach you sufficiently to your contemporaries may I here suggest to you to seek the society and conversation of ladies and gentlemen older than yourselves.[32]

> Adams enjoyed an old man's anecdotage—as in entertaining escorts when visiting the exhibition of Trumbull's painting, *The Declaration of Independence* at Faneuil Hall in December 1818, as reported in the press.

He well remembered, that, when engaged in signing the Declaration of Independence, a side conversation took place between Harrison, who was remarkably corpulent, and Elbridge Gerry, who was remarkably the reverse. "Ah, Gerry," said Harrison, "I shall have the advantage over you in this act."

"How so?" said Gerry.

"Why," replied Harrison, "when we come to be hung for this treason, I am so heavy, I shall plump down upon the rope and be dead in an instant; but you are so light, that you will be dangling and kicking about for an hour in the air. . . ."

He gave his warm approval to the picture as a correct rep-

Outliving Enemies

resentation of the Convention. "There is the door," said he, "through which Washington escaped when I nominated him as Commander-in-chief of the Continental Army!"[33]

As his eyes and hands failed, the grandchildren and neighbors' children would read to him. He grew excited as young neighbor Josiah Quincy read a passage in which Cicero looks upon death as a reunion with persons he had known and read about. Quincy acted as his Boswell.

That is just as I feel. Nothing would tempt me to go back. I agree with my old friend Dr. Franklin, who used to say on this subject,"We are all invited to a great entertainment. Your carriage comes first to the door; but we shall all meet there."[34]

Adams refused to disparage Franklin but would dredge up gossip about such other old foes as John Dickinson.

He gave me a great deal of trouble. His wife and mother were Quakers; and they constantly told him that he was ruining himself and his country by the measures he was advocating. If I had such a wife and mother, I should have been very unhappy; for I would have died rather than not have pursued the course I did.[35]

With more magnanimity, Adams would explain the grounds for quarreling so long with Jefferson.

I do not believe that Mr. Jefferson ever hated me. On the contrary, I believed he always liked me; but he detested Hamilton and my whole administration. Then he wished to be President of the United States, and I stood in his way. So he did everything that he could to pull me down. But if I should quarrel with him for that, I might quarrel with every man I have had anything to do with in life. . . . I forgive all my enemies and hope they may find mercy in heaven.[36]

Approaching age ninety, Adams was taken back sixty years

with a surprise visit from his first great passion, Hannah Quincy, twice since wed.

"What! Madam, shall we not go walk in Cupid's Grove together? . . ."

With a suspicion of girlish archness, she replied, "Ah, sir, it would not be the first time."[37]

When visited by very important persons, Adams could be eloquent as ever. When asked how he felt, he replied:

"I am not well. . . . I inhabit a weak, frail, decayed tenement; battered by the winds, and broken in upon by the storms; and from all I can learn, the landlord does not intend to repair."[38]

A new generation looked upon him as living history. A half-century earlier he had fought to establish the military academy. Now cadets from West Point paraded in his honor before his porch on a hot, humid August morning. Describing the scene, he bathed in "the milk of human kindness"—

They were drawn up in a body, before the piazza, listening to an old man, melting with heat, quaking with palsy, tormented with rheumatism and sciatica, and scarcely able to stand, uttering a few words—

"A desire of distinction is implanted by nature in every human bosom. . . . The great advantages you possess for attaining eminence in letters and science, as well as in arms . . . are a precious deposit, which you ought to consider as a sacred trust, for which you are responsible to your country and to a higher tribunal. These advantages, and the habits you have acquired, will qualify you for any course of life you may choose to pursue."—

The whole body marched up in a file, taking the old

Outliving Enemies

man by the hand; taking a final leave of him forever, and receiving his poor blessing.[39]

> Reminiscing with Judge Richard Peters, an old comrade from the revolutionary War Board, Adams declared peace with himself and with the world.

Theophrastus at ninety . . . is recorded to have said it was hard to go out of the world, when he had just learned to live in it. I am so far from his temper and his philosophy, that I think myself so well drilled and disciplined a soldier as to be willing to obey the word of command whenever it shall come, and in general or particular orders.[40]

> Upon learning that John Quincy, at age fifty-eight, had been named president, he was too overwhelmed for more than a father's blessing.

Never did I feel so much solemnity as upon this occasion. The multitude of my thoughts, and the intensity of my feelings are too much for a mind like mine, in its ninetieth year. May the blessing of God Almighty continue to protect you to the end of your life, as it has heretofore protected you in so remarkable a manner from your cradle![41]

> At ninety-one, when asked by Boston to comment on the approaching fiftieth birthday of Independence, Adams projected a future dependent on divine grace to ameliorate human error.

A memorable epoch in the annals of the human race; destined in future history to form the brightest or the blackest page, according to the use or the abuse of those political institutions by which they shall in time to come be shaped by the *human mind.*[42]

Adams on Adams

On the Fourth of July 1826, John Adams died "a few minutes before six in the evening."[43] His niece Louisa attended the deathbed. Close to his lips, she heard only "Thomas Jefferson."[44]

NOTES

INTRODUCTION. THE LAST ANGRY MAN

1. Charles Francis Adams, ed., *The Works of John Adams Second President of the United States*, vol. 2 (Boston: Little, Brown), 100.
2. Lester J. Cappon, ed., *Adams-Jefferson Letters*, vol. 2 (Chapel Hill: University of North Carolina Press, 1959), 525–26.
3. Mary A. Giunta et al., eds., *The Emerging Nation: A Documentary History of the Foreign Relations of the United States under the Articles of Confederation*, vol. 2 (Washington, D.C.: National Historical Publications and Records Commission, 1996), 42.
4. Alexander Biddle, ed., *Old Family Letters* (Philadelphia: Lippincott, 1892), 1: 296.
5. *Correspondence Between the Honorable John Adams and the Late William Cunningham* (Boston: E. M. Cunningham, 1823), 124.
6. Lyman H. Butterfield, ed., *Diary and Autobiography of John Adams*, vol. 1 (New York: Atheneum, 1964), lxix.
7. Peter Shaw, *The Character of John Adams* (Chapel Hill: University of North Carolina Press, 1976), 274.
8. *Works*, 10: 159.
9. Biddle, ed., *Old Family Letters*, 1: 105–6.
10. *Works*, 3: 197.
11. Ibid., 9: 612.
12. Carol Berkin, *Jonathan Sewall* (New York: Columbia University Press, 1974), 143.
13. Biddle, 1: 105–6.
14. *Works*, 3: 197.
15. *Works*, 9: 613.
16. Lawrence S. Mayo, ed., *History of . . . Massachusetts-Bay*, vol. 3 (Cambridge: Harvard University Press, 1936), 214.
17. Gilbert Chinard, *Honest John Adams* (Boston: Little, Brown, 1933), 161.

18. Guinta, ed., *Emerging Nation*, 2: 72.
19. Paul M. Zall, *Wit and Wisdom of the Founding Fathers* (Hopewell, N.J.: Ecco Press, 1996), 130.
20. Biddle, 2: 92.
21. Cappon, ed., *Adams-Jefferson Letters*, 2: 542.
22. Worthington C. Ford, ed., *Statesman and Friend: Correspondence of John Adams with Benjamin Waterhouse* (Boston: Little, Brown, 1927), 31.
23. Charles Francis Adams, ed., Correspondence Between John Adams and Mercy Warren, *Massachusetts Historical Society Collections*, 5s. 4: 490.
24. *Works*, 10: 53.
25. Daniel Webster, *Papers*, Charles M. Wiltse, ed., 1 (Hanover, N.H.: University Press of New England, 1974–1986), 375.
26. Ford, ed., *Writings of Thomas Jefferson* (New York: Putnam, 1892–1899), 10: 268.
27. L.F.S. Upton, ed., *Diary and Selected Papers of Chief Justice William Smith*, vol. 1 (Toronto: Champlain Society, 1963), 234.
28. *Works*, 3: 155.
29. Biddle, 2: 70.
30. Ibid., 64.
31. *Statesman and Friend*, 25–26.
32. Biddle, 2: 55.
33. Cappon, 2: 519.
34. John A. Schutz and Douglass Adair, eds., *The Spur of Fame: Dialogues of John Adams and Benjamin Rush, 1805–1813* (San Marino, Calif.: Huntington Library, 1966), 101.
35. Julian P. Boyd et al, eds., *Papers of Thomas Jefferson* (Princeton, N.J.: Princeton University Press, 1950–)11: 94–95.
36. Zall, *Wit and Wisdom*, 130.
37. Ibid., 97.
38. Ibid., 98.
39. Ibid., 118.
40. Charles Francis Adams, ed., *Letters of John Adams Addressed to His Wife* (Boston: Little, Brown, 1841), 207.
41. Ibid., 95–96.
42. George Whitney, *Some Account of Quincy* (Boston: Christian Repository, 1827), 53n.
43. *Spur of Fame*, 191.
44. *Letters to Wife*, 191.
45. Ibid., 197.

46. Donald H. Stewart, *Opposition Press of the Federalist Era* (Albany: State University of New York Press, 1969), 538.
47. Cappon, 2: 509.
48. *Works*, 10: 402.
49. below, 150

CHAPTER 1. BECOMING A LAWYER

1. Charles Francis Adams, *The Works of John Adams Second President of the United States*, vol. 10 (Boston: Little, Brown, 1856), 169.
2. Ibid., 9: 610.
3. Ibid., 1: 12n.
4. L.H. Butterfield, ed., *Diary and Autobiography of John Adams*, 4 vols. (Cambridge, Mass.: Harvard University Press, 1961), 3: 257.
5. *Works*, 9: 611.
6. Ibid., 10: 254.
7. Ibid., 9: 613.
8. Ibid., 10: 20.
9. Ibid., 2: 86.
10. George Whitney, *Some Account of the Early History of the Town of Quincy* (Boston: Christian Register Office, 1827), 52.
11. Clifford K. Shipton, ed., *Sibley's Harvard Graduates*, vol. 8 (Boston: Massachusetts Historical Society, 1933–1999), 448.
12. *Works*, 9: 610.
13. C.F. Adams, "Examinations for Harvard," *Proceedings of the Massachusetts Historical Society*, 2 s., vol. 14 (1901), 200–201.
14. *British Apollo*, 14–19 October (1709): 4.
15. Shipton, 13: 647.
16. Worthington C. Ford, ed., *Statesman and Friend: Correspondence of John Adams with Benjamin Waterhouse* (Boston: Little, Brown, 1927), 14.
17. *Works*, 10: 67–68.
18. C.F. Adams, "Examinations for Harvard," 200–201.
19. *Works*, 1: 41.
20. Shipton, *Sibley's Harvard Graduates*, 10: 346.
21. *Works*, 1: 41–42.
22. Ibid., 1: 36–37.
23. Ibid., 1: 38n.
24. Ibid., 1: 42.
25. Ibid., 9: 611.

26. "President in Search of a Profession," *The Month at Goodspeed's Book Shop,* vol. 19, no. 5 (February 1948), 134.
27. *Works,* 1: 42.
28. Ibid., 9: 611.
29. William S. Bartlet, ed., *The Frontier Missionary* (New York: Stanford and Swords, 1853), 10–12, 30.
30. *Works,* 1: 27.
31. Shipton, 13: 514–15.
32. Bartlet, facsimile between pp. 34 and 35.
33. *Works,* 2: 9–10.
34. Ibid., 2: 7n.
35. Ibid., 9: 611.
36. Ibid., 1: 43.
37. Ibid., 9: 611.
38. Ibid., 1:43.
39. Ibid., 9: 611–12.
40. Ibid., 2: 37.
41. Ibid., 2: 45–50.
42. Samuel Adams Drake, *Old Boston Taverns and Tavern Clubs* (Boston: Butterfield, 1917), 26–27.

CHAPTER 2. PRACTICING LAW

1. Henry Adams, *Birthplaces of Presidents John and John Quincy Adams* (Quincy, Mass.: Adams Memorial Society, 1936), 3.
2. Charles Francis Adams, *The Works of John Adams Second President of the United States,* vol. 2 (Boston: Little, Brown, 1856), 35–36.
3. Ibid, 2: 52–58.
4. Ibid., 2: 58n.
5. Ibid., 1: 59–60.
6. Ibid., 1: 47–48.
7. Ibid, 2: 118n.
8. Ibid, 9: 637.
9. Ibid., 10: 170.
10. Ibid., 4: 6.
11. Worthington C. Ford, ed., *Statesman and Friend: Correspondence of John Adams with Benjamin Waterhouse* (Boston: Little, Brown, 1927), 131–32.
12. *Works,* 2: 124n–125n.
13. Ibid., 2: 54–55.
14. Ibid., 2: 70.

15. C.F. Adams, ed., *Letters of Mrs. Adams*, 1 (Boston: Little, Brown, 1840), 6.
16. *Works*, 2: 128n.
17. John A. Schutz and Douglass Adair, eds., *The Spur of Fame: Dialogues of John Adams and Benjamin Rush, 1805–1813* (San Marino, Calif.: Huntington Library, 1966), 188.
18. *Works*, 2: 137–38.
19. Ibid., 2: 145.
20. Phyllis Levin, *Abigail Adams* (New York: St. Martins, 1987), 7, 496n.
21. L.H. Butterfield, ed., *Diary and Autobiography of John Adams*, vol. 2 (New York: Atheneum, 1964), 1: 108, 109.
22. Peter Shaw, *Character of John Adam* (Chapel Hill: University of North Carolina Press, 1976), 42n.
23. *Works*, 2: 145.
24. David Lee Child, "John Quincy Adams," *Homes of American Statesmen* (New York: Putnam, 1854), 304.

CHAPTER 3. BECOMING A RADICAL

1. Edith B. Gelles, *Portia* (Bloomington: Indiana University Press, 1992), 28.
2. Charles Francis Adams, ed., *The Works of John Adams Second President of the United States*, vol. 2 (Boston: Little, Brown, 1856), 146, 149.
3. Ibid., 1: 66.
4. Ibid., 2: 153.
5. Bernard Bailyn, *Ordeal of Thomas Hutchinson* (Cambridge, Mass.: Harvard University Press, 1974), 66.
6. Ibid., 375.
7. Thomas Hutchinson, *History of the Colony and Province of Massachusetts-Bay*, ed. Lawrence Shaw Mayo (Cambridge, Mass.: Harvard University Press, 1936), 3: 214.
8. *Works*, 2: 150–51.
9. *Works*, 2: 157.
10. Ibid., 2: 156.
11. Ibid., 2: 186.
12. Ibid., 2: 201.
13. John Rowe, "Extracts from the Diary of John Rowe," Edward L. Pierce, ed., *Proceedings of the Massachusetts Historical Society*, 2s. vol. 10 (1895), 62.
14. *Works*, 2: 195.

15. Ibid., 2: 210.
16. Ibid., 2: 210–11.
17. Ibid., 2: 213–14.
18. Ibid., 2: 215–16.
19. L. Kinvin Wroth and Hiller B. Zobel, eds., *Legal Papers of John Adams*, 3 vols. (Cambridge, Mass.: Harvard University Press, 1965), 2: 281.
20. Brooks Adams, "Convention of 1800 with France," *Proceedings of the Massachusetts Historical Society* 3s. 44(1910–11), 423–24.
21. *Legal Papers*, 2: 323.
22. *Works*, 2: 224n–226n.
23. *Spur of Fame*, 143.
24. *Works*, 2: 229–31.
25. John A. Schutz and Douglass Adair, eds., *The Spur of Fame: Dialogues of John Adams and Benjamin Rush, 1805–1813* (San Marino, Calif.: Huntington Library, 1966), 143.
26. *Works*, 2: 231–32.
27. Ibid., 2: 232.
28. Ibid., 2: 231.

CHAPTER 4. RECONCILING IDEA AND INCLINATION

1. Charles Francis Adams, ed., *The Works of John Adams Second President of the United States*, vol. 1 (Boston: Little, Brown, 1856), 113.
2. Ibid., 2: 317.
3. Ibid., 2: 255n.
4. Ibid., 2: 258.
5. Henry Adams, *Birthplaces of Presidents John and John Quincy Adams* (Quincy, Mass.: Adams Memorial Society, 1936), 6.
6. *Works*, 2: 264n.
7. Ibid., 2: 272.
8. Ibid.
9. Ibid., 2: 277.
10. Ibid, 2: 278–79.
11. Ibid., 2: 286.
12. Ibid., 2: 298.
13. Ibid., 2: 300–301.
14. Ibid.
15. Ibid., 2: 303–4.
16. Ibid., 2: 314.
17. Andrew Stephen Walmsley, *Thomas Hutchinson and the Ori-*

gins of the American Revolution (New York: New York University Press, 1999), 140–41.
  18. *Works*, 2: 312–13.
  19. Ibid., 2: 316.
  20. Ibid., 2: 328–31.
  21. Ibid., 9: 333.
  22. Ibid., 2: 323–24.
  23. Charles Francis Adams, ed., *Familiar Letters of John Adams to His Wife* (Boston: Little, Brown, 1841, 1876), 20.
  24. Ibid., 23.
  25. Ibid., 7.
  26. *Works*, 4: 8.
  27. Ibid., 9: 597–98.
  28. *Familiar Letters*, 17–18.
  29. *Works*, 2: 338.

CHAPTER 5. MANEUVERING INDEPENDENCE

  1. Frank Mumby, *George the Third and the American Revolution* (London: Constable, 1924), 346.
  2. *Works*, 2: 369, 370.
  3. Ibid., 2: 512n–513n.
  4. C.F. Adams, ed., *Familiar Letters of John Adams to His Wife* (New York: Hurd and Houghton, 1876), 31.
  5. Ibid., 39.
  6. Ibid., 66.
  7. Worthington C. Ford, ed., *Journals of the Continental Congress 1774–89*, vol. 1 (Washington, D.C.: GPO, 1904), 1: 32–37.
  8. Charles Francis Adams, ed., *The Works of John Adams Second President of the United States*, 2 (Boston: Little, Brown, 1856), 380.
  9. *Familiar Letters*, 40.
  10. Ibid., 42, 43, 45.
  11. *Works*, 2: 402, 403.
  12. Ibid., 9: 352.
  13. Ibid., 2: 405.
  14. Ibid., 2: 406.
  15. Peter Force, ed., *American Archives*, 4s. (Washington, D.C.: Clarke and Force, 1833) 2: 440.
  16. *Works*, 2: 406.
  17. *Familiar Letters*, 54–55.
  18. *Works*, 9: 356.

19. Ibid., 2: 406.
20. Ibid.
21. Ibid., 2: 407.
22. Ibid., 10: 79.
23. *Familiar Letters*, 84.
24. *Works*, 2: 408.
25. Milton E. Flower, *John Dickinson: Conservative Revolutionary* (Charlottesville: University Press of Virginia, 1983), 149.
26. *Familiar Letters*, 134.
27. *Works*, 10: 164.
28. Ibid., 2: 416-18.
29. *Familiar Letters*, 70.
30. Ibid., 2: 418–19.

CHAPTER 6. DECLARING INDEPENDENCE

1. Charles Francis Adams, ed., *The Works of John Adams Second President of the United States*, vol. 2 (Boston: Little, Brown, 1856), 419.
2. Ibid., 2: 423.
3. Edith B. Gelles, *Portia* (Bloomington: Indiana University Press, 1992), 32–33.
4. Worthington C. Ford, ed., *Statesman and Friend: Correspondence of John Adams with Benjamin Waterhouse* (Boston: Little, Brown, 1927), 134.
5. "Warren-Adams Letters," *Massachusetts Historical Society Collections* (Boston: Massachusetts Historical Society, 1917), 72: 117.
6. *Works*, 3: 22–23.
7. *Statesman and Friend*, 31.
8. Thomas Wendel, ed., *Thomas Paine's* Common Sense (Woodbury, N.Y.: Barron's, 1975), 98, 90.
9. *Works*, 2: 508–9.
10. *Works*, 2: 508.
11. Ibid., 509.
12. "Warren-Adams Letters," 72: 242-43.
13. Charles Francis Adams, *Familiar Letters of John Adams to His Wife* (New York: Hurd and Houghton, 1876), 146.
14. *Works*, 3: 24n.
15. Ibid., 3: 25n.
16. *Familiar Letters*, 149–50.
17. Ibid., 155.
18. *Works*, 2: 409–13.

19. "Warren-Adams Letters," 72: 242.
20. *Works*, 2: 513n.
21. Ibid., 2: 514n.
22. *Works*, 3: 68–69.
23. John A. Schutz and Douglass Adair, eds., *The Spur of Fame: Dialogues of John Adams and Benjamin Rush, 1805–1813* (San Marino, Calif.: Huntington Library, 1966), 159.
24. Mrs. George Ticknor in Charles M. Wiltse, ed., *Papers of Daniel Webster: Correspondence*, vol. 1 (Hanover, N.H.: University Press of New England, 1974–1986), 375.
25. *Spur of Fame*, 199.
26. *Works*, 2: 514n.
27. *Familiar Letters*, 193–94.
28. *Works*, 3: 69.
29. Ibid., 3: 70n.
30. Ibid., 3: 75–76.
31. Ibid., 3: 79–80.
32. Ibid., 3: 70n.

CHAPTER 7. PRACTICING DIPLOMACY

1. Charles Francis Adams, *The Works of John Adams Second President of the United States*, vol. 9 (Boston: Little, Brown, 1856), 405.
2. "Warren-Adams Letters," *Massachusetts Historical Society Collections* (Boston: Massachusetts Historical Society, 1917), 72: 264, 265.
3. Charles Francis Adams, *Familiar Letters of John Adams to His Wife* (New York: Hurd and Houghton, 1876), 228.
4. Kenneth Schaffel, "The American Board of War, 1776–1781," *Military Affairs* 50 (1986), 186.
5. Edith B. Gelles, *Portia* (Bloomington: Indiana University Press, 1992), 35.
6. *Familiar Letters*, 230.
7. *Works*, 3:91–92.
8. Ibid., 3: 97, 100–101, 105.
9. Ibid., 3: 109n.
10. Ibid., 3: 189–90.
11. Paul M. Zall, ed., *Wit and Wisdom of the Founding Fathers* (Hopewell, N.J.: Ecco Press, 1996), 110-11.
12. *Works*, 3: 167.
13. Edmund S. Morgan, *Benjamin Franklin* (New Haven, Conn.: Yale University Press, 2002), 280.

14. *Works*, 3: 139–43.
15. Ibid., 3: 155.
16. Zall, *Wit and Wisdom*, 96–97.
17. *Works*, 3: 147.
18. Peter Shaw, *The Character of John Adams* (Chapel Hill: University of North Carolina Press, 1976), 121.
19. *Works*, 3: 139.
20. *Familiar Letters*, 356, 357.
21. Shaw, *Character of John Adams*, 123.
22. Ibid., 125
23. *Familiar Letters*, 364.
24. Ibid., 364.
25. *Works*, 3: 228.
26. Ibid., 9: 618.
27. *Works* 3: 244.
28. Mary A. Giunta, *The Emerging Nation: A Documentary History of the Foreign Relations of the United States under the Articles of Confederation*, 1 (Washington, D.C.: National Historical Publications and Records Commission, 1996), 54–55.
29. Gilbert Chinard, *Honest John Adams* (Boston: Little, Brown, 1933), 161.
30. Giunta, *Emerging Nation*, 1: 95.
31. *Works*, 9: 618–19.
32. *Familiar Letters*, 380.

CHAPTER 8. BECOMING THE "WASHINGTON OF NEGOTIATION"

1. "Warren-Adams Letters," 2: 155, 156.
2. *Correspondence . . . in the Boston Patriot* (Boston: Everett and Munroe, 1809–1910), 430.
3. Ibid., 431, 387.
4. Ibid., 433–34.
5. Ibid., 149.
6. Ibid., 106.
7. Ibid., 571.
8. John Ferling, *John Adams: A Life* (Knoxville: University of Tennessee Press, 1992), 237–38.
9. Mary A. Giunta et al., eds., *The Emerging Nation: A Documentary History of the Foreign Relations of the United States under the Articles of Confederation*, 2 (Washington, D.C.: National Historical Publications and Records Commission, 1996), 24.

10. Giunta, *Emerging Nation*, 2: 42.
11. Charles Francis Adams, *The Works of John Adams Second President of the United States*, 9 (Boston: Little, Brown, 1856), 513–14.
12. *Correspondence in the Boston Patriot*, 433.
13. Giunta, 1: 630–31.
14. *Works*, 3: 359.
15. Ibid., 3: 303.
16. Ibid., 9: 618-19.
17. Ibid., 3: 306.
18. Ibid., 3: 300, 302.
19. Giunta, 2: 72.
20. Benjamin Franklin, *Writings*, Albert Henry Smyth, ed., 9 (New York: Macmillan, 1906), 62.
21. Ibid., 3: 336.
22. Lyman H. Butterfield, Marc Friedlander, and Mary-Jo Kline, eds., *The Book of Abigail and John* (Cambridge: Harvard University Press, 1975), 337.
23. *Works*, 9: 626.
24. Charles Francis Adams, *Letters of John Adams Addressed to His Wife* (Boston: Little, Brown, 1841) 2: 93, 95–96.
25. "Warren-Adams Letters," 2: 206.
26. Peter Shaw, *Character of John Adams* (Chapel Hill: University of North Carolina Press, 1976), 187.
27. "Warren-Adams Letters," 2: 209–11.
28. *Works*, 1: 403.
29. Ibid., 405–6.
30. Ibid., 1: 411, 412.
31. *Letters to His Wife*, 2: 104–5.
32. Ibid., 2: 106.
33. Abigail Adams Jr., *Journal and Correspondence*, Caroline A. DeWindt, ed. (New York: Wiley and Putnam, 1841) 1: ix.
34. Ibid., 1: viii.

CHAPTER 9. IMPLEMENTING INDEPENDENCE

1. Mary A. Giunta et al., eds. *The Emerging Nation: A Documentary History of the Foreign Relations of the United States under the Articles of Confederation*, 2 (Washington, D.C.: National Historical Publications and Records Commission, 1996), 606–7.
2. James B. Peabody, *John Adams: A Biography in His Own Words* (New York: Newsweek, Inc., 1973), 320.

3. Worthington C. Ford, ed., *Statesman and Friend: Correspondence of John Adams with Benjamin Waterhouse* (Boston: Little, Brown, 1927), 7.
4. Giunta, *Emerging Nation*, 2: 645.
5. L.F.S. Upton, ed., *Diary and Selected Papers of Chief Justice William Smith*, 1 (Toronto: Champlain Society, 1963), 234.
6. *Works*, 8: 256–58.
7. Ibid., 2: liv.
8. Lester J. Cappon, ed., *Adams-Jefferson Letters*, 1 (Chapel Hill: University of North Carolina Press, 1959), 228.
9. Charles Francis Adams, ed., *The Works of John Adams Second President of the United States*, 3 (Boston: Little, Brown, 1856), 392.
10. Ibid., 8: 372.
11. Cappon, ed., *Adams-Jefferson Letters*, 1: 121.
12. *Works*, 8: 355.
13. Ibid., 8: 243–44.
14. Ibid., 9: 623–24.
15. Ibid., 10: 53.
16. "Warren-Adams Letters . . . 1743–1814," *Massachusetts Historical Society Collections*, 2 (Boston: Massachusetts Historical Society, Collections 72 and 73, 1917–1925), 281.
17. *Works*, 3: 396.
18. "Warren-Adams Letters," 2: 277–78.
19. *Works*, 8: 437.
20. Ibid., 8: 434.
21. Ibid., 8: 452.
22. Ibid., 1: 438.
23. Ibid., 8: 478.
24. Ibid., 8: 474–75.
25. Peabody, *John Adams*, 327.
26. Abigail Adams Jr., *Journal and Correspondence*, Caroline A. DeWindt, ed., 2 (New York: Wiley and Putnam, 1841), 79.
27. Ibid., 2: 85.
28. Ibid., 2: 88–89.

Chapter 10. Succeeding Washington

1. Charles Francis Adams, ed., *Familiar Letters of John Adams to His Wife* (New York: Hurd and Houghton, 1876), 381.
2. Abigail Adams Jr., *Journal and Correspondence*, Caroline A. DeWindt, ed., 2 (New York: Wiley and Putnam, 1841), 87.

3. Charles Francis Adams, ed., *The Works of John Adams Second President of the United States*, 9 (Boston: Little, Brown, 1856), 556–57.
4. *Works*, 9: 557.
5. "Warren-Adams Letters . . . 1743–1814," *Massachusetts Historical Society Collections*, 2 (Boston: Massachusetts Historical Society, Collections 72 and 73, 1917–1925), 305.
6. Lester J. Cappon, ed., *Adams-Jefferson Letters*, 1 (Chapel Hill: University of North Carolina Press, 1959), 214.
7. Ibid, 9: 566.
8. Harold C. Syrett, ed., *Papers of Alexander Hamilton*, 27 vols. (New York: Columbia University Press, 1961–1987), 5: 247–48.
9. *Works*, 9: 567.
10. *Works*, 9: 564.
11. William Maclay, *Diary*, Kenneth R. Bowling and Helen Veit, eds., (Baltimore: Johns Hopkins University Press, 1988), 211.
12. Cappon, ed., *Adams-Jefferson Letters*, 1: 236.
13. William Maclay Diary. 33, 40.
14. *Works*, 8: 512–13,
15. Ibid., 1: 462.
16. Ibid., 6: 227.
17. Cappon, 1: 246.
18. Thomas Jefferson, *Papers of Thomas Jefferson*, Julian P. Boyd and Barbara Oberg et al., eds., 2 (Princeton, N.J.: Princeton University Press, 1950–), 20: 278.
19. *Works*, 8: 506, 508.
20. *Works*, 1: 460.
21. Ibid., 1: 465.
22. Ibid., 1: 467–68.
23. Charles Francis Adams, ed., *Letters of John Adams Addressed to His Wife* (Boston: Little, Brown, 1841), 2: 186.
24. *Works*, 1: 481.
25. *Letters to Wife*, 2: 134–35.
26. Ibid., 2: 189.
27. Ibid., 2: 191.
28. Ibid., 2: 197–98.
29. Ibid., 2: 202.
30. *Works*, 3: 422.
31. Ibid., 8: 535.
32. *Letters to Wife*, 2: 242.
33. *Works*, 1: 506–7.
34. *Letters to Wife*, 2: 207.

35. *Works*, 9: 47.
36. Worthington C. Ford, ed., *Statesman and Friend: Correspondence of John Adams with Benjamin Waterhouse* (Boston: Little, Brown, 1927), 64.
37. Ibid., 65
38. *Works*, 10: 47–48.
39. *Works*, 10: 42
40. Ibid., 9: 622.
41. Ibid., 9: 636.
42. Ibid., 9: 620.
43. Ibid., 1: 545.
44. *Letters to Wife*, 2: 257.
45. *Works*, 10: 152–53.
46. *Works*, 1: 544–45.
47. Ibid., 9: 578.
48. *Letters to Wife*, 2: 267.
49. *Works*, 1: 592.

Chapter 11. Outliving Enemies

1. John A. Schutz and Douglass Adair, eds., *The Spur of Fame: Dialogues of John Adams and Benjamin Rush, 1805–1813* (San Marino, Calif.: Huntington Library, 1966), 191.
2. Ibid., 263.
3. Alexander Biddle, ed., *Old Familiar Letters* (Philadelphia: Lippincott, 1892), 64.
4. Ibid., 146, 151.
5. Worthington C. Ford, ed., *Statesman and Friend: Correspondence of John Adams with Benjamin Waterhouse* (Boston: Little, Brown, 1927), 81.
6. Biddle, ed., *Old Familiar Letters*, 226.
7. Ibid., 55.
8. Charles Francis Adams, ed., *The Works of John Adams Second President of the United States*, 10 (Boston: Little, Brown, 1856), 264.
9. Ibid., 10: 395.
10. *Correspondence between John Adams and William Cunningham* (Boston: E.M. Cunningham, 1823), 124.
11. *Works*, 10: 159.
12. Biddle, ed., 105.
13. Peter Shaw, *Character of John Adams* (Chapel Hill: University of North Carolina Press, 1976), 274.

14. Charles Francis Adams, ed., "Correspondence between John Adams and Mercy Warren," *Massachusetts Historical Society Collections*, 5s, 4: 474.
15. *Works*, 10: 113, 153–54.
16. "Correspondence . . . Mercy Warren," 4: 471.
17. Biddle, 107.
18. Ibid., 296.
19. Ibid., 92.
20. Ibid., 156.
21. Henry S. Randall, *Life of Thomas Jefferson*, 3 (New York: Derby and Jackson, 1858), 639–40.
22. Lester J. Cappon, ed., *Adams-Jefferson Letters*, 2 (Chapel Hill: University of North Carolina Press, 1959), 293–94, 296.
23. Ibid., 609.
24. Ibid., 2: 353.
25. *Works*, 10: 229.
26. Ibid., 10: 213–14.
27. Cappon, 2: 529.
28. John Ferling, *John Adams: A Life* (Knoxville: University of Tennessee Press, 1992), 438.
29. Cappon, 2: 296.
30. *Statesman and Friend*, 152.
31. Thomas Jefferson, *Family Letters*, Edwin M. Betts and James A. Bear Jr., eds. (Columbia: University of Missouri Press, 1966), 464–65.
32. M.A. DeWolfe Howe, ed., *The Articulate Sisters* (Cambridge, Mass.: Harvard University Press, 1946), 25.
33. *Life of Josiah Quincy*, Edmund Quincy, ed. (Boston: Ticknor and Fields, 1867), 371.
34. Josiah Quincy, *Figures of the Past* (Boston: Roberts, 1883), 75.
35. Eliza Susan Quincy, ed., *Memoir of Eliza S.M. Quincy* (Boston: n.p., 1861), 188–89.
36. Josiah Quincy, *Figures of the Past*, 69.
37. Ibid., 57.
38. Charles W. March, *Reminiscences of Congress* (New York: Baker and Scribner, 1850), 2.
39. *Works*, 10: 401, 419–20.
40. Ibid., 10: 402.
41. Ibid., 10: 416.
42. Ibid., 10: 417.

43. Charles Francis Adams, ed., *Memoirs of John Quincy Adams* (Philadelphia, 1875), 7: 129.

44. Eliza Susan Quincy, ed., *Memoirs of Eliza S.M. Quincy,* 207n.

BIBLIOGRAPHY

Abbreviations of Primary Sources

The words of John Adams are excerpted principally from these collections referenced by abbreviation:

Adams-Warren	Adams, Charles Francis, ed. Correspondence between John Adams and Mercy Warren. *Massachusetts Historical Society Collections*, 5 ser. 4 (1878): 317–511.
Biddle	Biddle, Alexander, ed. *Old Family Letters*. 2 vols. Philadelphia: Lippincott, 1892.
Boston Patriot	*Correspondence in the Boston Patriot*. Boston: Everett and Munroe, 1809–1810.
Cappon	Cappon, Lester J., ed. *Adams-Jefferson Letters*. 2 vols. Chapel Hill: University of North Carolina Press, 1959.
Cunningham	*Correspondence Between the Honorable John Adams and the Late William Cunningham*. Boston: E. M. Cunningham, 1823.
Familiar Letters	Adams, Charles Francis, ed. *Familiar Letters of John Adams to His Wife*. New York: Hurd and Houghton, 1876.
Goodspeed's	"President in Search of a Profession." *The Month at Goodspeed's Book Shop*. Vol. 19, no. 5 (February 1948): 135.
Letters to Wife	Adams, Charles Francis, ed. *Letters of John Adams Addressed to His Wife*. Boston: Little, Brown, 1841.
Spur of Fame	Schutz, John A. and Douglass Adair, eds. *The Spur of Fame: Dialogues of John*

Bibliography

	Adams and Benjamin Rush, 1805–1813. San Marino, Calif.: Huntington Library, 1966.
Statesman and Friend	Ford, Worthington C., ed. *Statesman and Friend: Correspondence of John Adams with Benjamin Waterhouse.* Boston: Little, Brown, 1927.
Warren-Adams	"Warren-Adams Letters . . . 1743–1814." *Massachusetts Historical Society Collections.* 2 vols. Boston: Massachusetts Historical Society, Collections 72 and 73, 1917–1925.
Works	Adams, Charles Francis, ed. *The Works of John Adams Second President of the United States.* 10 vols. Boston: Little, Brown, 1856.

Works Cited

Adams, Abigail, Jr. *Journal and Correspondence.* 2 vols. Ed. by Caroline A. DeWindt. New York: Wiley and Putnam, 1841.

Adams, Brooks. "Convention of 1800 with France." *Proceedings of the Massachusetts Historical Society* 3 ser. 44 (1910–11): 377–428.

Adams, Charles Francis. "Examinations for Harvard." *Proceedings of the Massachusetts Historical Society* 2 ser. 14 (1901): 198–205.

Adams, C.F., ed., *Letters of Mr Adams*, 2 vols. Boston: Little, Brown, 1840.

Adams, C.F., ed., *Memoirs of John Quincy Adams.* Philadelphia, 1875.

Adams, Henry. *Birthplaces of Presidents John and John Quincy Adams.* Quincy, Mass.: Adams Memorial Society, 1936.

Bailyn, Bernard. *Ordeal of Thomas Hutchinson.* Cambridge, Mass.: Harvard University Press, 1974.

Bartlet, William S. *The Frontier Missionary.* New York: Stanford and Swords, 1953.

Berkin, Carol. *Jonathan Sewall.* New York: Columbia University Press, 1974.

Bowling, Kenneth R., and Helen Veit, eds. *Diary of William Maclay.* Baltimore: Johns Hopkins University Press, 1988.

Bibliography

Boyd, Julian P., ed. *Papers of Thomas Jefferson.* Princeton, N.J.: Princeton Unviersity Press, 1950–.

British Apollo. 14–19 October (1709): 4.

Butterfield, Lyman H., ed., *Diary and Autobiography of John Adams.* 4 vols. New York: Atheneum, 1964.

Butterfield, Lyman H., Marc Friedlander, and Mary-Jo Kline, eds., *The Book of Abigail and John.* Cambridge, Mass.: Harvard University Press, 1975.

Child, David Lee. "John Quincy Adams." *Homes of American Statesmen.* New York: Putnam, 1854.

Chinard, Gilbert. *Honest John Adams.* Boston: Little, Brown, 1933.

Drake, Samuel Adams. *Old Boston Taverns and Tavern Clubs.* Boston: Butterfield, 1917.

Ferling, John. *John Adams: A Life.* Knoxville: University of Tennessee Press, 1992.

Flower, Milton E. *John Dickinson, Conservative Revolutionary.* Charlottesville: University Press of Virginia, 1983.

Force, Peter, ed. *American Archives.* 4 ser. Washington, D.C.: Clarke and Force, 1833.

Ford, ed., *Writings of Thomas Jefferson,* 10 vols. New York: Putnam, 1892–1899.

Ford, Worthington C., ed. *Journals of the Continental Congress, 1774–1789.* 34 vols. Washington, D.C.: Government Printing Office, 1904.

Franklin, Benjamin. *Writings.* Edited by Albert Henry Smyth. 10 vols. New York: Macmillan, 1906.

Gelles, Edith B. *Portia.* Bloomington: Indiana University Press, 1992.

Giunta, Mary A. et al., eds. *The Emerging Nation: A Documentary History of the Foreign Relations of the United States under the Articles of Confederation.* 3 vols. Washington, D.C.: National Historical Publications and Records Commission, 1996.

Howe, M. A. DeWolfe, ed. *The Articulate Sisters.* Cambridge, Mass.: Harvard University Press, 1946.

Hutchinson, Thomas. *History of the Colony and Province of Massachusetts-Bay.* Edited by Lawrence Shaw Mayo. 3 vols. Cambridge, Mass: Harvard University Press, 1936.

Bibliography

Jefferson, Thomas. *Family Letters.* Edited by Edwin M. Betts and James A. Bear Jr. Columbia: University of Missouri Press, 1966.

———. *Papers of Thomas Jefferson.* Edited by Julian P. Boyd, Barbara Oberg, et al. 30 vols. (ongoing). Princeton, N.J.: Princeton University Press, 1950–.

Levin, Phyllis. *Abigail Adams.* New York: St. Martins, 1987.

Maclay, William. *Diary.* Edited by Kenneth R. Bowling and Helen Veit. Baltimore: Johns Hopkins University Press, 1988.

March, Charles W. *Reminiscences of Congress.* New York: Baker and Scribner, 1850.

Mayo, Lawrence S., ed. *History of . . . Massachusetts-Bay.* 3 vols. Cambridge, Mass.: Harvard University Press, 1936.

Morgan, Edmund S. *Benjamin Franklin.* New Haven, Conn.: Yale University Press, 2002.

Mumby, Frank. *George the Third and the American Revolution.* London: Constable, 1924.

Peabody, James B. *John Adams.* New York: Newsweek, 1973.

Quincy, Eliza Susan, ed. *Memoir of Eliza S.M. Quincy.* Boston: n.p., 1861.

Quincy, Josiah. *Figures of the Past.* Boston: Roberts, 1883.

———. *Life.* Edited by Edmund Quincy. Boston: Ticknor and Fields, 1867.

Randall, Henry S. *Life of Thomas Jefferson.* 3 vols. New York: Derby and Jackson, 1858.

Rowe, John. "Extracts from the Diary of John Rowe." Edited by Edward L. Pierce. *Proceedings of the Massachusetts Historical Society.* 2 ser. 10 (1895): 11–108.

Schaffel, Kenneth. "The American Board of War, 1776–78." *Military Affairs* 50 (1986): 185–89.

Shaw, Peter. *Character of John Adams.* Chapel Hill: University of North Carolina Press, 1976.

Shipton, Clifford K., ed. *Sibley's Harvard Graduates.* 18 vols. Boston: Massachusetts Historical Society, 1933–1999.

Smyth, Albert Henry, ed. *Writings of Benjamin Franklin.* 10 vols. New York: Macmillan, 1906.

Stewart, Donald H. *Opposition Press of the Federalist Era.* Albany: State University of New York Press, 1969.

Bibliography

Syrett, Harold C., ed. *Papers of Alexander Hamilton.* New York: Columbia University Press, 1961–1987.

Upton, L.F.S., ed. *Diary and Selected Papers of Chief Justice William Smith.* 2 vols. Toronto: Champlain Society, 1963.

Walmsley, Andrew Stephen. *Thomas Hutchinson and the Origins of the American Revolution.* New York: New York University Press, 1999.

Webster, Daniel. *Papers.* Edited by Charles M. Wiltse. 7 vols. Hanover, N.H.: University Press of New England, 1974–1986.

Wendel, Thomas, ed. *Thomas Paine's* Common Sense. Woodbury, N.Y.: Barron's, 1975.

Whitney, George. *Some Account of Quincy.* Boston: Christian Repository, 1827.

Zall, Paul M. *Wit and Wisdom of the Founding Fathers.* Hopewell, N.J.: Ecco Press, 1996.

Additional Resources

Davies, Kenneth Gordon. *Documents of the American Revolution, 1770–1783.* 21 vols. Dublin: Irish University Press, 1972–1981.

French, Allen. "The First George Washington Scandal." *Proceedings of the Massachusetts Historical Society* 65 (1935): 460–74.

Hutchinson, Thomas. *Diary and Letters.* Edited by Peter O. Hutchinson. 2 vols. London: Sampson, Low, 1886.

Stiles, Ezra. *Literary Diary.* Edited by Franklin Bowditch Dexter. 3 vols. New York: Scribners, 1901.

Zall, Paul M. *Jefferson on Jefferson.* Lexington: University Press of Kentucky, 2002.

INDEX

The abbreviation JA refers to John Adams; AA to his wife Abigail Adams

Adams, Abigail "Abby" (daughter of JA). *See* Smith, Abigail "Abby" Adams (daughter of JA)
Adams, Abigail (granddaughter of JA), 145
Adams, Abigail Smith (AA): on the British Court, 111–12; comes to Europe to join JA, 105; confidences to, by JA, 70; correspondence with JA, 52; dies of typhoid, 145; Hannah Quincy as match-maker for, 24; ill at home during JA inauguration, 128; illness of, 133; life with commuter JA, 44; loses baby Susanna, 37; on male-female relations, 71; married ten years, 27; meets JA, 26; miscarriage of child, 80–81; mother dies of dysentery, 67; moves in Boston, 37; relied on by JA, 39; returns to U.S., 119; secrets shared by JA, 53; stays in U.S. with JA in Europe, 82
Adams, Charles (son of JA): alcoholism of, 133; daughters of, 145; death of, 144; lives with aunt, 121–22; returns to Braintree, 95; siblings of, 27; travels to France, 89
Adams, Elihu, 68
Adams, John (British architect), 103
Adams, John (father of JA), 1, 24
Adams, John Quincy: in diplomatic career, 121; dispute with Jefferson, 124; education interrupted, 95; education of, 88; elected president, 149; in England, 102; in the Netherlands, 104; restores family finances, 137–38; returns to Europe, 89; returns to Harvard, 108; returns to Russia, 101; returns to U.S., 88; secretary to Dana, 95; secretary to JA, 105; siblings of, 27; travels to Europe, 31; travels to France, 82–83; travels to Russia, 95; travels to St. Petersburg, 101
Adams, Joseph (grandfather of JA), 1
Adams, Joseph (great-grandfather of JA), 1
Adams, Nancy (daughter-in-law), 145

173

Index

Adams, Samuel, 46–47, 55, 63, 75, 83
Adams, Susanna Boylston (mother of JA), 1, 24, 45, 133
Adams, Susanna (daughter of JA), 37
Adams, Susanna (granddaughter of JA), 145
Adams, Thomas (son of JA), 27, 44, 121
Alien and Sedition Acts, 132
Alliance (frigate), 87
alliances, 131
aristocracy, 62
Articles of Confederation, 77, 108, 113–14
Articles of War, 77

Bache, Benjamin, 138
Barbary States, 112
Bass, Joseph, 60
Bath, England, 102
Belcher, Moses, 2
Belcher, Mrs., 2
Bernard, Francis, 32
Boston (frigate), 82, 83
Boston, MA: court reopening petitioned, 30; evacuation of, 72; JA commutes to, 44; JA family moves to, 32, 46; JA health concerns by living in, 32
Boston Massacre, 37–39, 59
Boston Tea Party, 49
Boylston, Susanna. *See* Adams, Susanna Boylston (mother of JA)
Brattle, William, 47–48
Briant, Lemuel, 6

British Statutes at Large, 48–49
Brown, Andrew, 138
Bryant[*sic*], Lemuel, 2
Bunker's Hill (battle), 61, 64
Burr, Aaron, 134–35, 141

Callender, Alexander, 138
Carmarthen, Marquis, 109
Charlestown, MA, 64
civil rights, 34–36, 41, 75–76, 89
Cleverley, Joseph, 2, 9
Common Sense (Paine), 69
Congress: aristocracy in, 62; *Articles of Confederation*, 78; after Battle of Lexington, 60; committees within, 79–80; competency of delegates to, 53; conflicts within, 61–62, 72–74; daily business of, 58; debate on governmental form in, 69–70; establishes army, 63–64; First Continental session, 51; and independence concept, 56; Jefferson joins, 74–75; removes JA from France, 90; sends Dana to Russia, 95–101; sends JA abroad, 81–87, 89–97; sends JA home, 95–101; slavery views of, 76; Suffolk Resolves passed, 57
constitutions (*see also* writings of JA): congressional efforts in writing, 115; durability of, 129; of Massachusetts, 89, 114–15; preservation of, 49; privileges of, 52; of United States, 69, 115, 125; of various states, 69, 125

174

Index

Coolidge, Ellen, 146
Cooper, Samuel, 78
Copley, John Singleton, 22, 86, 103
Corbett, Michael, 34–35
Court of Inquisition, 47
Cushing, Thomas, 55

Deane, Silas, 85
Declaration of Independence, 75–76, 146–47
Defence of the Constitutions of the United States (JA), 69, 114
Democratic-Republicans, 126
Dickinson, John: aristocratic leader, 62; Articles of Confederation effort, 77; conflict with JA, 67, 72–73; efforts against independence, 64, 67; JA on, 147; militia colonel, 64; misses signing of Declaration of Independence, 76; obstructionist in Congress, 55; petitions King George III, 64, 72
Dickinson, Philemon, 62
Discourses on Davila (JA), 69, 124
Draper, Richard, 28–29
Dutch bankers, 93, 96, 118
Dutch Government: JA as negotiator to, 95; JA in conflict with Vergennes over, 94; U.S. recognition by, 93; U.S. treaty with, 97
dysentery, 67–68

early life of JA: ancestors and background, 1; celibacy of, 25–26; early education of, 2–4; at Harvard College, 4–9;
legal education of, 10–13, 28; military service of, 45, 62, 83
Elbridge, Gerry, 146
Ellsworth, Oliver, 130
England. *See* Great Britain
entangling alliances, 131
Esther (maid), 106

family life of JA: birth of son, Thomas, 44; in Braintree, 26, 122; care of sons, 95; children of, 27; death of brother Elihu, 68; death of daughter Abby, 144; death of daughter Susanna, 37; death of father, 24; death of mother, 24, 133; death of son Charles, 144; death of wife, 145; as farmer, 24–25, 138; as father of president, 149; grandchildren of, 145–46; on his three sons, 121–22; illness of son Charles, 133; illness of wife, 133; marries Abigail Smith, 26; meets Abigail Smith, 24, 26; moves to Boston, 32, 46; moves to Braintree, 42, 50; reunion with Abbey, 105–6
Farmers Letters (Dickinson), 62
Federalists, 69, 126, 131, 133–35
Fenno, John, 138
fevers: typhoid, 145; unspecified, 24, 60, 133; yellow, 138
Field (client), 16
finances of JA: inheritance, 24; restoration of, by son John Quincy, 137–38; sacrifices made, 81
Fisher, Miers, 55

Index

Fitch, Samuel, 27–28
Forrest, James, 39
France: Americans welcome in, 90; Franklin's plan for, 107; JA identity mistaken in, 83–84; JA sent to seek aid from, 81; revolutionary government for, 124; revolutionary ideas spread in U.S., 126; treaty with, 85; united with others against England, 98; U.S. alliance with, 96; U.S. dependency on, 90; U.S. peace with, 133, 141; U.S. war with, 132
Franklin, Benjamin: conflict with JA, 87, 93, 101–2; as described by JA, 99–100; feud with Lee, 85–86; meets Voltaire, 86–87; negotiates peace with Britain, 98; plan for French Parliament, 107, 114; quoted by JA, 138, 147; reviewed draft of Declaration of Independence, 76; single-legislature model, 107; as sole representative to France, 90; tricks JA in shared bedroom, 77–78
freedom of religion, 89
French Government: credit to, in America for Dutch loans, 97; influence of, in America, 90; as JA's intermediary, 94; JA's opinion of, 100; JA's policy criticism of, 90; Lee's opinion on, 87; new parliamentary structure for, 114; treatment of JA, 98–99
French language skills: of JA, 84, 86; of John Quincy Adams, 82, 88, 116
French revolution, 126–27, 132

Gaspée (revenue cutter), 46–47
Genet, Edmond ("Citizen"), 131
George III, King of England, 55, 108, 109–11
Germaine, Lord George, 90
Great Britain: Boston Tea Party response, 49; common laws of, 37; JA ambassador to, 107; JA tours, 116; smuggling laws of, 21; Stamp Act, 30; and Suffolk Resolves, 57; treaties with, 134; united forces against, 98; U.S. commercial treaty with, 89, 95; U.S. debt payment to, 132; U.S. peace treaty with, 98
Gridley, Jeremiah: advice to JA, 13, 23, 24; defends Writs of Assistance, 22; lawbook collection of, 47; patron to JA, 12; petitions reopening of Boston's Courts, 30; starts law club, 27–28

Hall, Mr., 45
Hall, Susanna Boylston Adams (mother of JA), 1, 24, 45, 133
Hamilton, Alexander: attacks on JA by, 134, 141; electoral votes for, 128; electoral voting maneuvers by, 123; JA on Jefferson's opinion of, 147; opinions of, by JA, 142; and Quasi War, 133; suspicion of, by JA, 131

Index

Hancock, John, 34, 60
Harrison, Benjamin, 146–47
health concerns of JA: Bath Spa visit for, 102; Braintree/Boston commute because of, 44; chest pains and malaise, 42; death of, 150; dysentery, 67–68; fears for, by living in Boston, 32; homesickness, 15; from labor and anxiety, 39; moves to Braintree because of, 11, 43; nervous pain, 130; from overwork, 44, 64; palsy, rheumatism, and sciatica, 148; palsy affliction, 143; in Philadelphia, 79–80; during presidency, 143; restored, back at farm, 128; Stafford Springs visit for, 43; from trip to Amsterdam, 105, 117
Hichborn, Benjamin, 73–74
History of the Rise, Progress, and Termination of the American Revolution (Warren, Mercy), 140
"Hobby Horse," 137
Holland: climate in, 117; JA efforts in, 98, 99
honors and dignitaries: biographies of, 139–40; meets ambassador from Tripoli, 112–13; meets King George III, 108–11; meets Lord Germaine, 90; meets Lord Richard Howe, 77–78; meets Louis XIV, 86; meets Luzerne, 88; meets Vergennes, 86; meets Willem V, 95; mistaken for Samuel Adams, 83–84; West Point cadets visit, 148
Hooper, Mr., 34
Howe, Lord Richard, 77
"Humphrey Ploughjogger," 28
Hutchinson, Thomas: avarice of, 30; JA triumphs over, 41; on judicial independence, 48–49; Parliament authority declared by, 46; Parliament authority disputed by JA, 47; popularity of, 43–44; Stamp Act and, 29; trial court with JA, 34, 35–36

impeachment, 48–49
impressment, 34–36
independence, 56, 73, 95, 98

Jay, John, 98, 100, 117, 127
Jefferson, Thomas: becomes vice president, 128; called to London, 118; conflict with JA, 124–25; *Declaration of Independence*, 75–76; Dutch loans, asks JA help on, 118–19; elected president, 134; impact on JA writing, 77; JA on, 147; JA writes to on terrorism, 131; loses presidency to JA, 128–29; meets JA, 74; reconciles with JA, 142–43; reputation of, 74; Sedition Act pardons, 132; on slavery, 76; writes preface to *Rights of Man*, 74; writings, 75
John Adams Street, 102–3
judicial independence, 48–49

177

Index

Judiciary Act, 135
justifiable homicide, 36

King, Richard, 49

La Luzerne, Chevalier de, 88
law practice of JA: beginnings of, 12–13, 15; as chief justice of Massachusetts, 68, 71; defense of John Hancock, 34; defense of Michael Corbett, 34–36; defense of Richard King, 49; defense of Thomas Preston, 39–40; early setbacks, 16–17; junto (law club) formation, 27–28
Lee, Arthur, 85, 87, 98
Lexington (battle), 59–60
Lincoln, Bela, 23
Lloyd, James, 141
Louis XIV, King of France, 86, 109
Luzac (professor), 95

Maccarty, Thaddeus, 8
Marsh, Joseph, 3–4
Marshall, John, 135
Mayhew, Joseph, 4–5, 9
Molineux, Sir Francis, 103
Montmorin, Madame de, 99
Morse, Jedediah, 139
"Mr. Insipid," 10
Murray, John (Lord Mansfield), 103

"Nabby". *See* Smith, Abigail "Abby" Adams (daughter of JA)
Noel, Nicholas, 82
"Novangulus," 59

Oliver, Andrew, 29
Oliver, Peter, 48
opinions of JA: on alcohol consumption, 20–21; on armed rebellion, 60; on *Articles of Confederation*, 77; on Battle of Lexington, 59–60; on Boston Massacre, 59; on constitutions, 114–15; on democracy, 70, 115–16; on equality, 124; on executive powers, 89; on France and French government, 98; on freedom of religion, 89; on Hamilton, 142; on monarchies, 124–25; on ostentatious display, 19; on Stamp Act, 28–30; on Tom Paine, 142
Osborne, Mr., 103
Oswald (British agent), 100
Otis, James, Jr.: effect of, on JA, 24; fought to reopen Boston courts, 30; fought Writs of Assistance, 21–22; on JA's military service, 45

Paine, Robert Treat, 55, 69–70, 125, 142
Panton, Lieutenant, 34–35, 36
paranoia, 87
Peace treaty, 98
Pestell (professor), 95
Peters, Richard, 149
pettifoggers, 16, 17
Pinckney, C.C., 128–29
Powel, Samuel, 55–56
presidential inauguration, 129–30
Preston, Thomas, 39, 40

Index

public official: Board of Ordnance, 79–80; board of supervisors, 28; in Congress, 51, 52–53, 55–69; on Congress, 62; in Congress, 70; Dutch loans to U.S., 91, 93, 96–97, 104, 118–19; Dutch negotiations, 95–97; Dutch recognition of U.S., 93; elected president, 127–29; elected to state legislature, 37; election as vice president, 123; as peace commissioner, 95; peace treaty, 98; presidential inauguration, 129–30; on promotion to advocate-general, 32–33; seeks loans in Holland, 91; surveyor of highways, 20
Putnam, James, 11
Putnam, Mrs., 11

Quasi War, 132
Quincy, Esther, 23
Quincy, Hannah, 22–23, 25, 26, 148
Quincy, John, 26
Quincy, Josiah (father of Hannah Quincy), 22
Quincy, Josiah (young neighbor), 147
Quincy, Samuel, 13

Reed, Joseph, 144
relationships: Hannah Quincy, 22–23, 25, 26, 148; with Jefferson, 125; meets Jefferson, 74; reconciliation with Jefferson, 142–43; to Sons of Liberty, 33, 56; with Washington, 123–24
Rights of Man (Paine), 124
Rush, Benjamin, 141–42, 143
Rutledge, Edward, 77

Savil, Elisha, 19
Savil, Mrs., 12
Sensible (frigate), 87, 89
Sewall, Jonathan, 21, 23, 32, 49–50
Shays's rebellion, 131
Sherman, Roger, 76
single-legislature model, 107
slavery, 75–76
Small, John, 33
Smith, Abigail. *See* Adams, Abigail Smith (AA)
Smith, Abigail "Abby" Adams (daughter of JA): corresponds with JA, 119; death of, by breast cancer, 144; first child born, 116; with JA in old age, 142; marriage of, 116; siblings of, 24; visits JA in Boston, 105
Smith, Caroline (granddaughter of JA), 145
Smith, John (grandson of JA), 145
Smith, Louisa (granddaughter of JA), 145, 150
Smith, William (father of AA), 19, 23, 26
Smith, William (grandson of JA), 145
Smith, William Stephen (son-in-law of JA), 116
smuggling, 21
Sons of Liberty, 33, 56
Spain, 134

Index

Spear, Samuel, 17
Stafford Springs, CT, 43
Stamp Act, 28–30
state constitutions, 68, 69, 114–15, 125
Stockbridge, Joseph, 5
Stone, Robert, 13
Suffolk Resolves, 57
Sullivan, John, 72
Summary Views of the Rights of British America (Jefferson), 75

terrorism, 131
Thomson, Charles, 62
Thoughts on Government (JA), 69, 70
tobacco, 113
travels of JA: to Amsterdam, 104; to Bath, England, 102; to France, 81–83; in Paris, 81–83, 84–87; to Paris, 89–90; Paris Mission, 90; in Paris with family, 107; in Philadelphia, 55, 60–69; returns to U.S., 118–19; in Spain, 89
treaties, 114; Articles of Confederation and, 114; with Britain, 89, 95, 98, 100–101, 102, 108; with England, 134; with France, 85, 133; with Holland, 93, 97, 99; Jay Treaty, 132; with Spain, 134
Tripoli, 112
Tucker, Samuel, 83

U.S. constitution, 69, 115, 125
U.S. Navy, 133–34

Vauguyon, Duke de la, 94

Vergennes, Charles Gravier: advises JA on conduct, 90; calls JA for peace conference, 95; cuts off JA, 90; hosts JA, 98–99; letters to, from JA, 87; meets JA, 86; on the power of the press, 132; receives credit for Dutch treaty, 97; suspicion of, by JA, 94, 101, 102
Voltaire, 86

Warren, James, 73–74
Warren, Joseph, 33, 61, 64
Warren, Mercy Otis, 140
Washington, George: advised JA on national defense, 133; city named after, 135; commander in chief nomination, 63–64, 147; elected president, 123; endorses JA as successor, 127; escorted by JA, 64; at JA inauguration, 129–30; radical attacks on, 127; threatened by mobs, 131
Watson, Brook, 110
West, Benjamin, 103, 104
Willard, Nahum, 10
Willem V, Stadtholder, 95, 109
writings of JA: *Articles of War*, 77; autobiography, 140–43; *Defence of the Constitutions of the United States*, 69, 114; *Discourses on Davila*, 69, 124; *Dissertation on the Canon and Feudal Law*, 28; on General William Brattle, 47–49; as "Hobby Horse," 137; as "Humphrey Ploughjogger,"

Index

28; as "Novangulus," 59; reply to Hutchinson, 46–47; on state constitution, 68; *Thoughts on Government*, 69

writs of assistance, 21

Yorke, Sir Joseph, 96

www.ingramcontent.com/pod-product-compliance
Lightning Source LLC
Chambersburg PA
CBHW020738230426
43665CB00009B/475